CALEB ROSS

ASP NET Core 7.0 and Angular 16 Development

Copyright © 2024 by Caleb Ross

All rights reserved. No part of this publication may be reproduced, stored or transmitted in any form or by any means, electronic, mechanical, photocopying, recording, scanning, or otherwise without written permission from the publisher. It is illegal to copy this book, post it to a website, or distribute it by any other means without permission.

First edition

This book was professionally typeset on Reedsy.
Find out more at reedsy.com

Contents

Introduction	1
Chapter 1: Setting Up Your Development Environment	9
Chapter 3	18
Chapter 3: Building Angular 16 Applications	25
Chapter 4: Managing State with Angular and ASP.NET Core	38
Chapter 5: Routing in Angular	55
Chapter 6: User Authentication and Authorization	69
Chapter 8: Testing Angular Applications	95
Chapter 9: Deployment Strategies for Angular Applications	133
Chapter 10: Advanced Topics in Angular Development	143
Chapter 11: Mastering Angular Testing Techniques	161
Chapter 12: Deploying Angular Applications	178
Chapter 13: Advanced Angular Development Techniques	189
Chapter 14: Security Best Practices for Angular Applications	209
Chapter 15: Building and Maintaining High-Performance...	218
Conclusion	230

Introduction

The Need for Full-Stack Development with ASP.NET Core and Angular
In today's fast-paced, technology-driven world, web application development has become a critical skill for building modern, scalable, and responsive applications. Businesses and organizations of all sizes are increasingly relying on web-based systems to serve their customers, streamline operations, and foster collaboration across teams and stakeholders. This growing demand for robust, user-friendly, and high-performance web applications underscores the importance of full-stack development, a methodology that covers both the frontend (client-side) and backend (server-side) aspects of an application.

Full-stack development is not just a buzzword but a comprehensive skill set that allows developers to work on every component of a web application, from the user interface to the database, from the business logic to deployment and maintenance. This ability to handle the full spectrum of development tasks provides several key benefits, including flexibility, greater control over the development process, and the ability to work independently or in smaller, more agile teams.

At the core of modern full-stack development are two powerful and widely used frameworks: **ASP.NET Core** on the backend and **Angular** on the frontend. These technologies provide a robust foundation for developing dynamic, scalable, and secure web applications, leveraging the best practices in software architecture, data management, and user experience design.

The Value of Full-Stack Development

Before diving into the specific tools—ASP.NET Core and Angular—it's important to understand the inherent value of full-stack development in the broader web development ecosystem. Full-stack developers are increasingly in demand because they have the ability to take ownership of entire projects, from concept to completion. This holistic approach ensures that developers can craft solutions that are well-integrated, reducing bottlenecks that arise when responsibilities are siloed between frontend and backend teams.

In many organizations, full-stack developers are seen as problem solvers who can bridge gaps between design, functionality, and scalability. This versatility reduces dependency on multiple teams and offers significant cost and time savings, particularly for startups or small businesses that may not have the resources to hire specialized developers for each layer of the application.

Furthermore, full-stack development provides:

- **Enhanced Collaboration**: Full-stack developers can easily communicate across different teams, improving collaboration between UI/UX designers, backend engineers, and other stakeholders.
- **Improved Debugging and Maintenance**: A full understanding of both client and server-side code makes it easier for developers to debug issues and optimize application performance.
- **Better Project Management**: Full-stack developers have a comprehensive view of the application, making it easier to identify risks, plan features, and manage project timelines effectively.
- **Career Flexibility**: Full-stack development skills are highly transferable across industries, giving developers the flexibility to work in diverse environments or transition between frontend and backend roles as needed.

By mastering **ASP.NET Core 7.0** and **Angular 16**, developers can position themselves as highly versatile, in-demand professionals capable of building modern web applications that meet the needs of today's users.

Why Choose ASP.NET Core and Angular for Full-Stack Development?

INTRODUCTION

There are numerous web development technologies available, but the combination of **ASP.NET Core** for backend development and **Angular** for frontend development stands out due to their scalability, robustness, and ability to meet the complex requirements of modern applications.

- **ASP.NET Core**: ASP.NET Core is a modern, open-source web framework developed by Microsoft. It is designed to build cross-platform applications that can run on Windows, macOS, and Linux. ASP.NET Core offers an exceptional framework for developing APIs, server-side logic, and data-driven applications, leveraging Microsoft's extensive ecosystem of tools and libraries. ASP.NET Core is known for its high performance, reliability, and security features, making it a go-to choice for enterprises and developers looking to build scalable applications.
- **Angular**: Angular, developed and maintained by Google, is a highly popular frontend framework for building dynamic, single-page applications (SPAs). Angular offers a rich set of tools, a powerful templating engine, and features that streamline the process of building modern web user interfaces. With a strong emphasis on maintainability, testability, and performance, Angular enables developers to create highly interactive applications with clean code and reusable components.

Together, **ASP.NET Core** and **Angular** represent a powerful duo for full-stack development. ASP.NET Core handles server-side logic, APIs, data access, and security, while Angular excels at creating responsive, dynamic user interfaces and handling client-side tasks. Combining these frameworks allows developers to build cohesive, full-stack applications where both the backend and frontend are seamlessly integrated.

Overview of ASP.NET Core 7.0 and Angular 16

What is ASP.NET Core 7.0?

ASP.NET Core is a high-performance, cross-platform web framework designed by Microsoft to build modern, cloud-based, internet-connected applications. Whether you're developing web apps, RESTful APIs, or microservices, ASP.NET Core 7.0 offers unparalleled flexibility and performance.

ASP.NET Core is part of the larger .NET ecosystem, meaning it benefits from a vast library of tools and technologies that make it easier to implement complex functionalities, such as authentication, database management, and real-time communication.

ASP.NET Core 7.0 builds on the strengths of previous versions, offering even better performance, scalability, and developer experience. It continues to support cross-platform development, meaning you can write code that runs on Windows, Linux, or macOS without changing the core architecture of your application.

Key Features of ASP.NET Core 7.0:

- **Cross-Platform**: Develop and deploy your application on any major operating system.
- **Performance**: ASP.NET Core consistently ranks as one of the fastest web frameworks available today.
- **Unified Platform**: Use one framework for web, desktop, mobile, cloud, and more.
- **Minimal APIs**: Simplified APIs for quickly developing microservices and small apps.
- **Middleware**: Highly customizable request pipelines that make it easy to add or remove features.
- **Dependency Injection**: Built-in support for dependency injection ensures a modular, testable codebase.
- **Real-Time Communication**: Integrated support for **SignalR** to build real-time apps like chat systems or live dashboards.

ASP.NET Core 7.0 further optimizes the framework's performance and scalability, making it ideal for large-scale applications and enterprise solutions. Its tight integration with cloud technologies, particularly Microsoft's own Azure platform, makes it an excellent choice for developers building scalable cloud-native applications.

INTRODUCTION

What is Angular 16?

Angular is a TypeScript-based frontend web application framework developed by Google. It's widely used for creating single-page applications (SPAs) due to its robust set of features, including two-way data binding, dependency injection, and a component-based architecture.

Angular 16 continues the evolution of the framework with key updates focused on improving performance, developer experience, and reducing the complexity of building modern web applications. Angular emphasizes reusability, testability, and maintainability, which are crucial aspects of enterprise-level software.

Key Features of Angular 16:

- **Component-Based Architecture**: Modular design makes it easy to manage, test, and reuse components.
- **Reactive Forms and Observables**: Use RxJS for handling asynchronous events and building reactive, data-driven interfaces.
- **Routing and Navigation**: Angular's Router makes building SPAs seamless and ensures smooth transitions between views.
- **Standalone Components**: Angular 16 introduces standalone components that don't require NgModules, simplifying module management.
- **Improved Hydration for Server-Side Rendering (SSR)**: Angular Universal's performance has been improved, making server-side rendered apps more efficient.
- **Typescript Integration**: Leverage the power of TypeScript to write cleaner, type-safe code.
- **Material Design Components**: Angular Material provides a rich set of UI components for building professional and visually appealing user interfaces.

Angular 16 maintains backward compatibility with previous versions, making it easier for developers to upgrade their applications without significant rewrites. It also includes optimizations for faster build times and better rendering performance, ensuring that applications run efficiently across a wide range of devices.

Together, ASP.NET Core 7.0 and Angular 16 provide an incredibly powerful combination of server-side and client-side technologies that enable developers to build complex, feature-rich web applications with ease.

Key Differences from Previous Versions

ASP.NET Core 7.0 vs. ASP.NET Core 6.0

While ASP.NET Core 6.0 introduced significant improvements, such as minimal APIs, ASP.NET Core 7.0 further refines these features with performance enhancements, improved developer experience, and new tools for handling microservices and cloud-native applications.

Here are some of the key updates in ASP.NET Core 7.0:

- **Performance Optimizations**: ASP.NET Core 7.0 includes several under-the-hood optimizations, making it even faster for both development and production environments. The framework is more efficient in handling high volumes of requests and offers better memory management.
- **Improved Minimal APIs**: Building on the introduction of minimal APIs in ASP.NET Core 6.0, version 7.0 streamlines the process even further by making it easier to create lightweight, fast APIs with minimal configuration.
- **Security Enhancements**: ASP.NET Core 7.0 improves security features, particularly around authentication, OAuth, and JWT tokens, ensuring better protection for API endpoints and user data.
- **Unified .NET Development**: ASP.NET Core 7.0 continues the unification of the .NET ecosystem, providing developers with more consistent tools and libraries across different platforms and workloads.

Angular 16 vs. Angular 15

Angular 16 introduces several notable improvements and new features, particularly focused on developer productivity, performance, and reducing the complexity of managing large-scale applications.

INTRODUCTION

Key updates in Angular 16 include:

- **Standalone Components**: One of the most significant changes in Angular 16 is the introduction of standalone components. These components no longer need to be declared within an NgModule, simplifying the management of Angular applications, especially in large codebases.
- **Server-Side Rendering Enhancements**: Angular 16 improves the hydration process, making server-side rendered applications faster and more efficient.
- **TypeScript Improvements**: Angular 16 supports TypeScript 5.0, which brings new language features and better performance, ensuring that Angular apps can benefit from the latest advances in TypeScript development.
- **Router Improvements**: Angular's router has been updated to improve navigation performance and reduce memory overhead, providing a smoother user experience in SPAs.

These updates make Angular 16 a more developer-friendly, high-performance framework that can easily handle the growing demands of modern web applications.

What You Will Learn in This Book

This book is designed to provide a comprehensive, hands-on guide to full-stack development using **ASP.NET Core 7.0** and **Angular 16**. Whether you're a seasoned developer looking to upgrade your skills or a beginner interested in entering the world of full-stack development, this book will equip you with the knowledge and tools needed to build scalable, modern web applications.

Throughout the course of this book, you will:

- **Set Up a Full-Stack Development Environment**: Learn how to configure and set up your development environment using the latest tools, including Visual Studio, Visual Studio Code, Node.js, and the Angular CLI.
- **Build a RESTful API with ASP.NET Core**: Understand how to create a

robust, secure API using ASP.NET Core 7.0, covering everything from basic routing to advanced API features such as GraphQL and gRPC.
- **Develop Dynamic Frontend Applications with Angular 16**: Master Angular's component-based architecture, build dynamic forms, manage state, and navigate between views using Angular Router.
- **Handle Authentication and Security**: Learn how to secure your applications using industry-standard practices such as JWT authentication, OAuth, and role-based access control in both the frontend and backend.
- **Optimize Application Performance**: Discover the best practices for optimizing the performance of both ASP.NET Core APIs and Angular frontend applications, including techniques like lazy loading, caching, and optimizing database queries.
- **Deploy Your Applications to the Cloud**: Get hands-on experience deploying your applications to cloud platforms like Azure, AWS, or Docker, and learn how to set up continuous integration/continuous deployment (CI/CD) pipelines.
- **Build Real-Time Applications**: Explore how to use SignalR and WebSockets to create real-time communication features such as live chat, notifications, or collaborative editing tools.
- **Architect Microservices-Based Applications**: Dive into microservices architecture with ASP.NET Core and learn how to design, build, and deploy scalable microservice applications with Angular as the frontend.

By the end of this book, you will be fully equipped to build, test, deploy, and maintain full-stack applications using ASP.NET Core 7.0 and Angular 16, giving you the skills to excel in today's competitive development landscape.

Chapter 1: Setting Up Your Development Environment

Full-stack development with ASP.NET Core 7.0 and Angular 16 requires a properly configured development environment to facilitate seamless integration between frontend and backend. This chapter will guide you step-by-step through setting up your environment, including the necessary prerequisites, installation of essential software, and the creation of your first project. Having the right tools and configurations will enable you to build, test, and deploy high-performance applications effectively.

Prerequisites for ASP.NET Core 7.0 and Angular 16

Before diving into installation and setup, it's important to ensure that you meet the necessary prerequisites for working with ASP.NET Core 7.0 and Angular 16. Depending on your operating system and environment, you may need to install specific tools to ensure compatibility and efficiency during the development process.

1. Operating System

ASP.NET Core 7.0 is cross-platform, meaning it can run on various operating systems, including:

- **Windows**: Supported versions include Windows 10 or higher.
- **macOS**: Versions 10.15 or higher (Catalina or newer) are recommended.

- **Linux**: ASP.NET Core can be installed on various Linux distributions, including Ubuntu, Fedora, and CentOS.

Angular 16 is also platform-agnostic and works well on all operating systems that support **Node.js** and **NPM** (Node Package Manager).

2. Hardware Requirements

While full-stack development doesn't require heavy hardware resources, having a reasonably powerful machine is essential for smooth operation and quick build times. The following specs are recommended:

- **RAM**: At least 8 GB, with 16 GB being optimal for handling multiple running services and compiling projects.
- **Storage**: SSD drives are highly recommended as they significantly improve speed when installing and running packages.
- **Processor**: A multi-core processor (4+ cores) will speed up build processes and development operations, particularly when running Angular builds and ASP.NET Core services simultaneously.

3. Development Tools

To work effectively with ASP.NET Core 7.0 and Angular 16, the following tools are required:

- **.NET SDK 7.0**: The .NET 7.0 Software Development Kit (SDK) allows you to develop, build, and run .NET applications. Ensure you download the version specific to your operating system.
- **Node.js**: Node.js is the runtime environment for JavaScript, required for running Angular and its CLI (Command Line Interface). Make sure to install Node.js version 16.0 or later.
- **NPM**: Node Package Manager comes bundled with Node.js and is used for managing JavaScript dependencies, including Angular libraries and modules.
- **Visual Studio or Visual Studio Code**: These Integrated Development Environments (IDEs) are essential for writing, testing, and debugging

your code.

In addition to these prerequisites, it's essential to have a reliable internet connection to download packages and dependencies during the installation process.

Installing Visual Studio and Visual Studio Code

The next step in your development setup is installing the appropriate IDE. For ASP.NET Core, **Visual Studio** is a robust and fully integrated development environment tailored for .NET applications. However, if you prefer a lightweight, cross-platform editor, **Visual Studio Code (VS Code)** is an excellent alternative.

1. **Installing Visual Studio (for Windows/Mac)**

Visual Studio is ideal for ASP.NET Core projects as it includes powerful tools for debugging, profiling, and working with databases, and it seamlessly integrates with .NET.

Steps to Install Visual Studio:

1. **Download Visual Studio**: Navigate to Visual Studio's official website. Select either the **Community** edition (free for individual developers, open-source projects, and academic use) or **Professional/Enterprise** editions for more advanced features.
2. **Run the Installer**: Once the download completes, run the installer. The installation wizard will guide you through the process.
3. **Select Workloads**:

- Choose the **ASP.NET and web development** workload. This option will automatically install the .NET Core SDK, the tools for ASP.NET, and other essential web development components.
- If you plan to work on Azure-based applications, you can also select the **Azure development** workload to install tools and services specific to Azure.

1. **Installation**: After selecting the required workloads, proceed with the installation. Depending on your internet speed and selected components, this process may take some time.
2. **Launch Visual Studio**: Once the installation is complete, open Visual Studio and sign in with your Microsoft account to enable additional features like cloud services, extensions, and GitHub integration.

Visual Studio Setup for macOS:

For macOS users, you can also download **Visual Studio for Mac** from the same website. The steps are similar, and the macOS version includes support for ASP.NET Core and Azure but is optimized for Apple's ecosystem.

2. Installing Visual Studio Code (Cross-Platform)

If you're looking for a more lightweight and flexible option, **Visual Studio Code** (VS Code) is a powerful code editor that works across all platforms (Windows, macOS, Linux) and can be extended with a variety of plugins to support both ASP.NET Core and Angular development.

Steps to Install Visual Studio Code:

1. **Download VS Code**: Visit Visual Studio Code's official site and download the version suitable for your operating system.
2. **Install VS Code**: Run the installer and follow the instructions for your platform.
3. **Install Extensions**:

- To develop ASP.NET Core projects, install the **C# Extension**. Go to the **Extensions** panel on the left sidebar (or press Ctrl+Shift+X), search for "C#", and click **Install**.
- For Angular development, install the **Angular Snippets** and **Angular Language Service** extensions to enable syntax highlighting, intellisense, and auto-completion.

VS Code is widely appreciated for its flexibility, making it an excellent option for both .NET and Angular development.

CHAPTER 1: SETTING UP YOUR DEVELOPMENT ENVIRONMENT

Setting Up Node.js, NPM, and Angular CLI

Angular 16 is a client-side framework built on JavaScript (or more accurately, TypeScript). To manage dependencies and compile your Angular project, you'll need to install **Node.js** and **NPM**. Afterward, you can install the **Angular CLI** (Command Line Interface), which simplifies the development and scaffolding of Angular projects.

1. Installing Node.js and NPM

Node.js is a runtime that allows JavaScript to be executed outside of a web browser. NPM (Node Package Manager) comes bundled with Node.js and helps manage packages and libraries in JavaScript projects.

Steps to Install Node.js and NPM:

1. **Download Node.js**: Go to the official Node.js website and download the **LTS (Long-Term Support)** version. This is the most stable version and is recommended for most development purposes.
2. **Run the Installer**: Follow the installation instructions for your operating system.
3. **Verify Installation**: After installation, verify that both Node.js and NPM are correctly installed by running the following commands in your terminal or command prompt:

```bash
Copy code
node -v
npm -v
```

1. These commands should return the version numbers of Node.js and NPM, confirming that the installation was successful.

2. Installing Angular CLI

The **Angular CLI** is an essential tool that allows you to create, build, test, and manage Angular projects efficiently.

Steps to Install Angular CLI:

1. **Install Angular CLI Globally**: Open your terminal or command prompt and run the following command:

```bash
Copy code
npm install -g @angular/cli
```

1. The -g flag ensures that Angular CLI is installed globally on your system, meaning you can use the ng command from any directory.
2. **Verify Installation**: Once installed, you can verify the Angular CLI installation by running:

```bash
Copy code
ng version
```

1. This will display information about the installed version of Angular CLI, as well as the versions of Angular and Node.js.

Creating Your First ASP.NET Core and Angular Project

With your environment set up, it's time to create your first full-stack project. We will use **Visual Studio** for ASP.NET Core and **Angular CLI** for Angular 16.

1. **Creating an ASP.NET Core Project**

Steps to Create an ASP.NET Core Web API:

CHAPTER 1: SETTING UP YOUR DEVELOPMENT ENVIRONMENT

1. **Open Visual Studio**: Launch Visual Studio and select **Create a new project** from the start page.
2. **Select ASP.NET Core Web API**: In the project template list, choose **ASP.NET Core Web API** and click **Next**.
3. **Configure Your Project**: Provide a **Project Name**, **Location**, and **Solution Name**. Click **Next**.
4. **Select .NET Version**: In the next window, select **.NET 7.0** as the framework version.
5. **Enable HTTPS and Docker (Optional)**: You can enable HTTPS and Docker support for your project if desired.
6. **Create Project**: Click **Create** to generate the ASP.NET Core Web API project.

Your project is now created, and you can see the default file structure in the **Solution Explorer**. Visual Studio automatically sets up controllers, routes, and a basic API.

2. Creating an Angular Project

Now that the backend is set up, let's create the Angular frontend project. Steps to Create an Angular Application:

1. **Open Terminal**: Open a terminal window and navigate to the directory where you want to create your Angular project.
2. **Create Angular App**: Run the following command to create a new Angular project:

```bash
Copy code
ng new my-angular-app
```

1. The Angular CLI will prompt you to choose certain options:

- Choose **Yes** for Angular routing (this sets up routing for your SPA).
- Select **CSS** or another style format based on your preference.

1. **Navigate to Project Directory**: Once the project is created, navigate into your new Angular project:

```bash
Copy code
cd my-angular-app
```

1. **Start Development Server**: To verify the installation, start the Angular development server by running:

```bash
Copy code
ng serve
```

1. Open your browser and go to http://localhost:4200/ to see your Angular app running.

At this point, you have two separate projects—an **ASP.NET Core Web API** and an **Angular SPA**. In later chapters, we will cover how to integrate them to create a unified full-stack application.

Structuring Your Development Workspace

A well-structured development workspace is key to managing code efficiently and avoiding confusion as your project grows. Both ASP.NET Core and Angular offer flexible options for organizing your code, allowing you to follow best practices that ensure maintainability and scalability.

1. Folder Structure for ASP.NET Core

A typical ASP.NET Core project has a predefined folder structure, but you can extend it based on your project's complexity.

- **Controllers**: Contains API controllers that handle HTTP requests.
- **Models**: Contains the data models or entities that represent the application's data.
- **Data**: Contains database-related code, such as DbContext classes and database migrations.
- **Services**: Business logic services that handle operations outside of the controllers.
- **Migrations**: If you're using Entity Framework Core, database migrations will be stored here.

Additionally, you can create other folders like **Repositories** and **DTOs (Data Transfer Objects)** to organize your project further.

2. Folder Structure for Angular

Angular applications are modular and component-based, so organizing the project structure is critical for scalability.

- **app**: Contains all your application components, services, modules, and routes.
- **components**: Folder to store reusable components (e.g., navigation, headers).
- **services**: Folder for services responsible for handling API calls or business logic.
- **modules**: Organize your application into feature modules for better management.
- **assets**: Folder for storing static assets like images, icons, and styles.

Maintaining a clean folder structure will make it easier to manage both your backend and frontend code as your application evolves.

Chapter 3

Chapter 2: Building a Basic ASP.NET Core Web API

ASP.NET Core 7.0 is a modern, high-performance web framework designed to build scalable web applications and APIs. One of the most common use cases for ASP.NET Core is building RESTful APIs, which serve as the backend for many types of applications, including web apps, mobile apps, and IoT devices. This chapter focuses on creating and configuring your first ASP.NET Core Web API, understanding the essentials of REST, and connecting your API to a database using **Entity Framework Core**. By the end of this chapter, you'll have a functional API that can be tested with tools like Postman.

Introduction to RESTful APIs

REST (Representational State Transfer) is an architectural style that defines a set of constraints for creating scalable web services. A RESTful API uses HTTP requests to perform operations on data, such as retrieving, updating, creating, or deleting resources. ASP.NET Core provides powerful tools to create RESTful APIs, making it an ideal platform for building backend services that can interact with multiple clients.

1. REST Principles

To fully understand the power of RESTful APIs, it's important to grasp the principles that guide this architectural style:

1. **Statelessness**: Each API request from a client must contain all the information needed to process it. The server does not store any session data between requests. This simplifies scalability because each request is treated independently.
2. **Client-Server Separation**: REST emphasizes a clear separation between the client (frontend) and the server (backend). The client should not need to understand the server's business logic, and the server doesn't need to know about the client's UI.
3. **Uniform Interface**: REST APIs provide a uniform way of interacting with resources using standard HTTP methods:

- **GET**: Retrieve a resource.
- **POST**: Create a new resource.
- **PUT**: Update an existing resource.
- **DELETE**: Remove a resource.

1. **Resource Identification through URIs**: Each resource in a RESTful API is identified by a URI (Uniform Resource Identifier). For example, in an e-commerce application, a product might be accessed via /api/products/1.
2. **Stateless Communication via HTTP**: RESTful APIs rely on HTTP as the communication protocol. This makes it easy to interact with web browsers, mobile apps, and other clients that already use HTTP.
3. **Use of HTTP Status Codes**: RESTful APIs return appropriate HTTP status codes in response to requests:

- 200 OK: The request was successful.
- 201 Created: A new resource was successfully created.
- 400 Bad Request: The client sent an invalid request.
- 404 Not Found: The requested resource could not be found.
- 500 Internal Server Error: The server encountered an error.

2. **Why RESTful APIs?**
REST has become the dominant architecture for web APIs because it is

simple, scalable, and widely supported. With ASP.NET Core, you can quickly develop RESTful APIs that can serve as the backbone of your applications. Here are some reasons why RESTful APIs are ideal for modern web development:

- **Platform Independence**: RESTful APIs are not tied to any specific technology stack, allowing you to build APIs in .NET that can be consumed by Angular, React, iOS, Android, or any other platform.
- **Scalability**: Because REST is stateless, it's easier to scale APIs horizontally by adding more servers to handle increased load.
- **Simplicity**: The reliance on HTTP methods and status codes makes RESTful APIs straightforward to implement and use.

Now that you have a foundational understanding of REST, we'll move on to creating your first ASP.NET Core Web API.

Creating and Configuring Your First Web API

In this section, we will build a simple API for managing a list of products. The API will allow users to perform basic operations such as retrieving all products, getting a specific product, adding new products, updating existing ones, and deleting products.

1. **Project Setup**

   Step 1: Create a New ASP.NET Core Web API Project

   1. **Open Visual Studio** and select **Create a new project** from the start page.
   2. In the **Create a new project** dialog, select **ASP.NET Core Web API** and click **Next**.
   3. Configure your project:

   - **Project Name**: ProductAPI
   - **Location**: Choose a directory for your project.
   - **Solution Name**: ProductAPISolution
   - Click **Next**.

1. In the next window, select **.NET 7.0** as the framework. Leave the other options as default, then click **Create**.

Visual Studio will create a new Web API project with a default structure. You'll see several folders like **Controllers**, **Models**, and **Properties**, which we'll use to organize our code.

Step 2: Understand the Default Structure

Your newly created project will have the following default structure:

- **Controllers**: Contains API controllers, which handle incoming HTTP requests and return responses.
- **Program.cs**: This file configures the application and is responsible for setting up middleware, services, and routing.
- **appsettings.json**: This is the configuration file where you can store settings such as database connection strings.
- **LaunchSettings.json**: Contains configuration settings for launching the application (i.e., ports, environment variables, etc.).

Controllers, Routing, and Middleware in ASP.NET Core

In ASP.NET Core, API controllers are responsible for defining the API endpoints, handling incoming HTTP requests, and returning responses. Let's dive deeper into how controllers, routing, and middleware work together to create a functional API.

1. Controllers

A **Controller** in ASP.NET Core is a class that handles HTTP requests and returns appropriate HTTP responses. In the context of a Web API, controllers are responsible for exposing endpoints that allow clients to interact with resources.

Creating a Product Controller

Let's create a new controller to handle product-related actions:

1. In the **Controllers** folder, right-click and select **Add > New Item**.

2. Select **API Controller - Empty** and name it ProductsController.cs.
3. Inside ProductsController.cs, create the following basic structure:

```csharp
Copy code
using Microsoft.AspNetCore.Mvc;

namespace ProductAPI.Controllers
{
    [ApiController]
    [Route("api/[controller]")]
    public class ProductsController : ControllerBase
    {
        // In-memory list of products for demonstration
        private static List<Product> products = new List<Product>
        {
            new Product { Id = 1, Name = "Laptop", Price = 1000 },
            new Product { Id = 2, Name = "Phone", Price = 600 }
        };

        // HTTP GET: api/products
        [HttpGet]
        public ActionResult<IEnumerable<Product>> GetProducts()
        {
            return Ok(products);
        }
    }

    public class Product
    {
        public int Id { get; set; }
        public string Name { get; set; }
        public decimal Price { get; set; }
    }
}
```

Here's a breakdown of what's happening:

- **[ApiController]**: This attribute designates the class as a controller for a

Web API.
- **[Route("api/[controller]")]**: This attribute defines the base route for all actions in the controller. The [controller] token will be replaced with the controller name (Products), resulting in /api/products.
- **GetProducts()**: This method handles HTTP GET requests and returns a list of products.

2. Routing

Routing in ASP.NET Core defines how HTTP requests are mapped to the controller actions. There are two main types of routing:

- **Attribute Routing**: Routes are defined directly in the controller using attributes like [Route] or [HttpGet].
- **Convention-Based Routing**: Routing is defined globally in Program.cs using a central routing table.

In our example, we use **attribute routing**, which gives us more control over the routes for individual actions.

Defining Routes for Specific Actions

In addition to the GET method for retrieving all products, we can define routes for specific actions like retrieving a product by ID or adding a new product:

```csharp
Copy code
// HTTP GET: api/products/{id}
[HttpGet("{id}")]
public ActionResult<Product> GetProductById(int id)
{
    var product = products.FirstOrDefault(p => p.Id == id);
    if (product == null)
    {
        return NotFound();
    }
```

```
    return Ok(product);
}

// HTTP POST: api/products
[HttpPost]
public ActionResult<Product> CreateProduct(Product product)
{
    product.Id = products.Max(p => p.Id) + 1;
    products.Add(product);
    return CreatedAtAction(nameof(GetProductById), new { id =
    product.Id }, product);
}
```

Here's what these methods do:

- **GetProductById(int id)**: This action retrieves a specific product by its ID. The id parameter is extracted from the route.
- **CreateProduct(Product product)**: This action allows clients to add a new product. It returns a 201 Created response, which is the standard HTTP status code for successful resource creation.

3. Middleware

Middleware is a core part of the ASP.NET Core request pipeline. Middleware components are responsible for handling HTTP requests and responses. Middleware can be used for logging, authentication, error handling, and more.

In your Program.cs file, you'll find some default middleware components that are already configured:

```csharp
Copy code
var builder = WebApplication.CreateBuilder(args);
```

Chapter 3: Building Angular 16 Applications

Angular is a widely-used, open-source web application framework maintained by Google, designed to simplify the development of single-page applications (SPAs). With Angular, developers can build dynamic and interactive user interfaces with ease. Angular 16 introduces several powerful features that streamline application development and enhance performance, making it an excellent choice for frontend development in full-stack applications.

In this chapter, we will explore Angular's core architecture, learn how to create and manage components, use two-way data binding and directives, understand dependency injection, and communicate effectively with an ASP.NET Core API. By the end of this chapter, you will have a solid understanding of Angular's architecture and how to develop Angular-based frontends that interact seamlessly with backend APIs.

Understanding Angular Architecture

To build applications effectively with Angular, it is important to understand its architecture. Angular is a component-based framework that provides a structured approach to building web applications by breaking down the application into reusable components, services, and modules.

1. Core Concepts of Angular Architecture

Angular's architecture revolves around several key concepts:

- **Modules**: Angular applications are divided into modules. A module is a container for related components, services, directives, and pipes. Every Angular application has at least one root module (called AppModule), which bootstraps the application.
- **Components**: Components are the building blocks of Angular applications. Each component controls a portion of the user interface (UI) and includes both logic (via the component class) and template (HTML for the UI).
- **Templates**: A template defines the view of a component. Angular uses HTML templates and extends them with directives and data binding to dynamically render content.
- **Services**: Services are classes that handle business logic, data retrieval, or other tasks that components can share. They are usually injected into components via **Dependency Injection (DI)**.
- **Directives**: Directives are special markers on elements in a template that tell Angular to do something with that element (e.g., show, hide, or modify the element).
- **Data Binding**: Angular supports different types of data binding, allowing data to flow between the component's class and its template (UI).

2. Angular Application Structure

Here's a typical folder structure for an Angular application:

- **src/**: The main source code directory, containing:
- **app/**: The application module, components, services, and routing.
- **assets/**: Static assets like images, icons, or stylesheets.
- **environments/**: Configuration files for different environments (e.g., production, development).
- **app.module.ts**: The root module of the Angular application.
- **main.ts**: The entry point of the application where Angular bootstraps the app.
- **index.html**: The root HTML file that loads the Angular application.

Each component, service, and module is organized into folders, making it easier to maintain and scale the application. Now that we've covered the basic structure, let's dive into creating and managing Angular components.

Setting Up and Creating Angular Components

Angular applications are built around components, each responsible for a specific piece of the user interface. Components are composed of three main parts:

- **The Component Class**: Defines the logic and behavior of the component.
- **The Template**: Defines the view (HTML) that the component displays.
- **The Style**: Defines the CSS styles specific to the component.

1. Setting Up an Angular Project

To begin, we need to set up an Angular project using the Angular CLI (Command Line Interface). Follow these steps to create a new Angular project:

Step 1: Install Angular CLI

If you haven't already installed Angular CLI, run the following command:

```bash
Copy code
npm install -g @angular/cli
```

Step 2: Create a New Angular Application

Once the CLI is installed, create a new Angular project by running:

```bash
Copy code
ng new my-angular-app
```

During project creation, you'll be prompted to select options such as whether to add routing (choose Yes) and the stylesheet format (CSS is recommended). After project creation, navigate into your project directory:

```bash
Copy code
cd my-angular-app
```

Step 3: Serve the Application

To verify that the setup is correct, run the Angular development server using the following command:

```bash
Copy code
ng serve
```

Open your browser and go to http://localhost:4200/ to see the default Angular app running.

2. Creating a Component

Now that the application is set up, let's create a component. Angular CLI provides commands to generate components easily.

Step 1: Generate a Component

To generate a new component named ProductList, run the following command:

```bash
Copy code
ng generate component product-list
```

This command creates four files in the src/app/product-list/ folder:

- product-list.component.ts: The component class that defines the logic.
- product-list.component.html: The template file that defines the view (UI).
- product-list.component.css: The CSS file that contains styles for the component.
- product-list.component.spec.ts: A test file for unit testing the component.

Step 2: Understanding the Component

Here's a basic breakdown of what the product-list.component.ts file looks like:

```typescript
Copy code
import { Component } from '@angular/core';

@Component({
  selector: 'app-product-list',
  templateUrl: './product-list.component.html',
  styleUrls: ['./product-list.component.css']
})
export class ProductListComponent {
  products = [
    { id: 1, name: 'Laptop', price: 1000 },
    { id: 2, name: 'Phone', price: 600 },
    { id: 3, name: 'Tablet', price: 400 }
  ];
}
```

- **@Component**: This decorator indicates that the class is an Angular component. It takes an object with properties like selector, templateUrl, and styleUrls.
- **selector**: Defines the custom HTML element for this component (<app-product-list>).
- **templateUrl**: Points to the HTML template that defines the view.
- **styleUrls**: Points to the CSS file that contains styles for this component.

The component's class contains a products array, which stores a list of products. This data will be displayed in the template.

Step 3: Update the Template

Now let's modify the product-list.component.html file to display the list of products:

```html
Copy code
<h2>Product List</h2>
<ul>
  <li *ngFor="let product of products">
    {{ product.name }} - ${{ product.price }}
  </li>
</ul>
```

- ***ngFor**: This is a structural directive that repeats the li element for each item in the products array. It binds each product to the product variable, which is used to display the product name and price.

Finally, add the <app-product-list> tag to app.component.html (the root component template) to display the ProductList component on the page:

```html
Copy code
<app-product-list></app-product-list>
```

Save the changes and check your browser at http://localhost:4200/. You should now see the list of products displayed.

Two-Way Data Binding and Directives

Data binding is one of Angular's most powerful features, allowing seamless communication between the component class (TypeScript) and the template (HTML). There are several types of data binding in Angular, including interpolation, property binding, event binding, and two-way data binding.

1. **Types of Data Binding**

- **Interpolation**: Allows you to display data from the component class in the template. Example: {{ product.name }}

- **Property Binding**: Binds an element's property to a value in the component class. Example: [disabled]="isDisabled"
- **Event Binding**: Binds an event (e.g., click) to a method in the component class. Example: (click)="onClick()"
- **Two-Way Data Binding**: Syncs data between the component class and the template. Angular uses [(ngModel)] for two-way data binding, making it easy to update both the view and the model simultaneously.

2. Using Two-Way Data Binding

Two-way data binding is useful when building forms or other interactive components where the UI needs to reflect changes in the component class and vice versa.

To demonstrate two-way data binding, let's modify our product list to allow users to update product names.

Step 1: Import FormsModule

To use two-way data binding, we need to import FormsModule into app.module.ts:

```typescript
Copy code
import { FormsModule } from '@angular/forms';

@NgModule({
  declarations: [
    AppComponent,
    ProductListComponent
  ],
  imports: [
    BrowserModule,
    FormsModule
  ],
  providers: [],
  bootstrap: [AppComponent]
})
export class AppModule { }
```

Step 2: Add Two-Way Data Binding in the Template

In product-list.component.html, add an input field bound to the product.name property using two-way data binding:

```html
Copy code
<ul>
  <li *ngFor="let product of products">
    <input [(ngModel)]="product.name" /> - ${{ product.price }}
  </li>
</ul>
```

Now, whenever the user edits the product name in the input field, the changes are immediately reflected in the component's products array.

3. Directives in Angular

Directives are special markers in the DOM that Angular uses to apply logic to elements and components. There are three types of directives:

- **Structural Directives**: Alter the structure of the DOM (e.g., *ngFor, *ngIf).
- **Attribute Directives**: Change the appearance or behavior of an element (e.g., [ngClass], [ngStyle]).
- **Custom Directives**: You can create custom directives to encapsulate reusable logic.

We've already seen *ngFor in action. Another commonly used structural directive is *ngIf, which conditionally renders an element based on a boolean expression.

For example, we can show a message if there are no products in the list:

```html
Copy code
<p *ngIf="products.length === 0">No products available</p>
```

Dependency Injection and Services in Angular

Dependency Injection (DI) is a design pattern where a class receives its dependencies from an external source rather than creating them itself. In Angular, services are injected into components using DI, making it easy to share data and functionality across different parts of the application.

1. Creating a Service

Services in Angular are used for business logic, data retrieval, and other tasks that can be shared among components. Let's create a ProductService to manage product data.

Step 1: Generate the Service

To generate a new service, run the following command:

```bash
Copy code
ng generate service product
```

This creates a product.service.ts file in the src/app/ directory. Update the service as follows:

```typescript
Copy code
import { Injectable } from '@angular/core';

@Injectable({
  providedIn: 'root'
})
export class ProductService {
  products = [
    { id: 1, name: 'Laptop', price: 1000 },
    { id: 2, name: 'Phone', price: 600 },
    { id: 3, name: 'Tablet', price: 400 }
  ];

  getProducts() {
```

```
    return this.products;
  }

  addProduct(product: any) {
    this.products.push(product);
  }
}
```

The ProductService contains methods for retrieving and adding products. The @Injectable() decorator makes the service available for DI.

Step 2: Inject the Service into the Component

Now, inject the ProductService into the ProductListComponent:

```typescript
Copy code
import { Component } from '@angular/core';
import { ProductService } from '../product.service';

@Component({
  selector: 'app-product-list',
  templateUrl: './product-list.component.html',
  styleUrls: ['./product-list.component.css']
})
export class ProductListComponent {
  products: any[] = [];

  constructor(private productService: ProductService) {
    this.products = this.productService.getProducts();
  }
}
```

Here's what happens:

- The ProductService is injected into the component via the constructor.
- The products array is populated by calling the getProducts() method of the service.

This setup allows the ProductService to manage product data, while the ProductListComponent is responsible for rendering the UI.

Communicating with the ASP.NET Core API

In a full-stack application, the Angular frontend communicates with the ASP.NET Core backend via HTTP requests. Angular provides the HttpClient module to make it easy to send HTTP requests and handle responses.

1. Setting Up HttpClientModule

To communicate with an API, you first need to import the HttpClientModule into your app.module.ts:

```typescript
Copy code
import { HttpClientModule } from '@angular/common/http';

@NgModule({
  declarations: [
    AppComponent,
    ProductListComponent
  ],
  imports: [
    BrowserModule,
    FormsModule,
    HttpClientModule
  ],
  providers: [],
  bootstrap: [AppComponent]
})
export class AppModule { }
```

The HttpClientModule enables Angular to send HTTP requests and handle responses.

2. Sending an HTTP GET Request

Let's modify the ProductService to fetch products from an ASP.NET Core API:

```typescript
import { Injectable } from '@angular/core';
import { HttpClient } from '@angular/common/http';
import { Observable } from 'rxjs';

@Injectable({
  providedIn: 'root'
})
export class ProductService {
  private apiUrl = 'https://localhost:5001/api/products'; // ASP.NET Core API URL

  constructor(private http: HttpClient) { }

  getProducts(): Observable<any[]> {
    return this.http.get<any[]>(this.apiUrl);
  }
}
```

Here's how it works:

- The HttpClient service is injected into ProductService.
- The getProducts() method sends an HTTP GET request to the ASP.NET Core API and returns an observable.

3. Updating the Component to Use the API

Finally, update the ProductListComponent to use the API:

```typescript
import { Component, OnInit } from '@angular/core';
import { ProductService } from '../product.service';

@Component({
  selector: 'app-product-list',
```

```
  templateUrl: './product-list.component.html',
  styleUrls: ['./product-list.component.css']
})
export class ProductListComponent implements OnInit {
  products: any[] = [];

  constructor(private productService: ProductService) { }

  ngOnInit(): void {
    this.productService.getProducts().subscribe(data => {
      this.products = data;
    });
  }
}
```

- The ngOnInit() lifecycle hook is used to fetch products from the API when the component initializes.
- The subscribe() method listens for data from the observable and updates the products array.

Now, when you run the Angular application, it will fetch products from the ASP.NET Core API and display them in the UI.

Chapter 4: Managing State with Angular and ASP.NET Core

In modern web applications, managing state effectively is crucial for delivering a responsive and user-friendly experience. State management involves handling the data that determines how the application behaves and what it displays at any given time. In this chapter, we will explore state management in Angular applications and how it interacts with ASP.NET Core backends. We will cover various approaches to state management, including using RxJS and Observables, implementing NgRx for advanced state management, and strategies for persisting state in ASP.NET Core using sessions and cookies. Additionally, we will discuss best practices for synchronizing state between the frontend and backend.

Introduction to State Management

State management refers to the way we handle the data that represents the current status of an application. In a single-page application (SPA) built with Angular, the state can include various pieces of information, such as user authentication status, form data, or the contents of a shopping cart.

Effective state management is essential for:

- **User Experience**: Providing users with a seamless and intuitive experience

as they interact with the application.
- **Performance**: Ensuring that the application responds quickly to user actions without unnecessary data fetching or processing.
- **Maintainability**: Making it easier to manage and update the application as it grows in complexity.

In Angular, state management can be accomplished through various approaches, including:

- **Local Component State**: Each component can manage its own state using class properties.
- **Services**: Services can store and manage shared state, allowing multiple components to access and modify the same data.
- **State Management Libraries**: Libraries like NgRx provide a more structured approach to managing state across larger applications.

Using RxJS and Observables in Angular

RxJS (Reactive Extensions for JavaScript) is a library for reactive programming using Observables, which allow you to work with asynchronous data streams. Observables provide a powerful way to manage state and handle asynchronous data in Angular applications.

1. Understanding Observables

An Observable is a data type that represents a stream of values over time. Observables can emit multiple values, and you can subscribe to them to receive updates. Observables are particularly useful for handling asynchronous operations such as HTTP requests, user input events, and more.

Example of Creating an Observable:

To create a simple Observable in Angular, you can use the following code:

```
typescript
Copy code
```

```
import { Observable } from 'rxjs';

const observable = new Observable<string>(subscriber => {
  subscriber.next('Hello, world!');
  subscriber.complete();
});

observable.subscribe({
  next: value => console.log(value),
  complete: () => console.log('Observable completed')
});
```

In this example:

- An Observable is created that emits a single string value, "Hello, world!".
- The subscribe() method is used to listen for emitted values and handle completion.

2. Using RxJS with HTTP Requests

In Angular, the HttpClient service returns Observables, allowing you to work with the asynchronous nature of HTTP requests. This makes it easy to manage state when retrieving data from an API.

Example of Making an HTTP Request with Observables:

In your ProductService, you can fetch products from the ASP.NET Core API using RxJS Observables:

```typescript
Copy code
import { Injectable } from '@angular/core';
import { HttpClient } from '@angular/common/http';
import { Observable } from 'rxjs';

@Injectable({
  providedIn: 'root'
})
export class ProductService {
```

CHAPTER 4: MANAGING STATE WITH ANGULAR AND ASP.NET CORE

```
  private apiUrl = 'https://localhost:5001/api/products';

  constructor(private http: HttpClient) {}

  getProducts(): Observable<Product[]> {
    return this.http.get<Product[]>(this.apiUrl);
  }
}
```

By returning an Observable from the getProducts() method, you can subscribe to it in your components:

```
typescript
Copy code
import { Component, OnInit } from '@angular/core';
import { ProductService } from '../product.service';
import { Product } from '../product.model';

@Component({
  selector: 'app-product-list',
  templateUrl: './product-list.component.html',
  styleUrls: ['./product-list.component.css']
})
export class ProductListComponent implements OnInit {
  products: Product[] = [];

  constructor(private productService: ProductService) {}

  ngOnInit(): void {
    this.productService.getProducts().subscribe(data => {
      this.products = data;
    });
  }
}
```

In this code:

- The ngOnInit() lifecycle hook subscribes to the getProducts() Observable and updates the products array with the fetched data.

3. Handling State with Observables

Using Observables to manage state in Angular allows you to respond to changes in data dynamically. You can create subjects (a special type of Observable) to manage state across components.

Example of Using BehaviorSubject:

You can use a BehaviorSubject to keep track of the current user:

```typescript
Copy code
import { Injectable } from '@angular/core';
import { BehaviorSubject, Observable } from 'rxjs';

@Injectable({
  providedIn: 'root'
})
export class AuthService {
  private currentUserSubject: BehaviorSubject<User | null> = new BehaviorSubject<User | null>(null);

  constructor() {}

  getCurrentUser(): Observable<User | null> {
    return this.currentUserSubject.asObservable();
  }

  setCurrentUser(user: User): void {
    this.currentUserSubject.next(user);
  }
}
```

In this example:

- The AuthService maintains a BehaviorSubject for the current user. The getCurrentUser() method returns an Observable that components can subscribe to, allowing them to react to changes in the user's state.

Managing Application State with NgRx

As Angular applications grow in complexity, managing state can become challenging. NgRx is a state management library that provides a Redux-inspired pattern for managing application state in Angular applications. It offers a robust and scalable approach to managing complex states by utilizing actions, reducers, effects, and a central store.

1. Installing NgRx

To get started with NgRx, you first need to install the necessary packages. Run the following command in your Angular project:

```bash
Copy code
ng add @ngrx/store @ngrx/effects @ngrx/store-devtools
```

This command adds NgRx Store, NgRx Effects, and NgRx Store DevTools to your project.

2. Understanding NgRx Concepts

NgRx is built around several core concepts:

- **Store**: A centralized state management container that holds the application state.
- **Actions**: Objects that represent a change in state. Actions are dispatched to the store to trigger state changes.
- **Reducers**: Pure functions that take the current state and an action as inputs and return a new state.
- **Selectors**: Functions that allow you to query specific slices of state from the store.
- **Effects**: Classes that handle side effects, such as asynchronous operations like HTTP requests.

3. Setting Up NgRx Store

To set up NgRx Store, follow these steps:

Step 1: Create the State Model

First, define your state model for products:

```typescript
Copy code
export interface Product {
  id: number;
  name: string;
  price: number;
}

export interface AppState {
  products: Product[];
}
```

Step 2: Create Actions

Create actions to represent state changes. Create a file called product.actions.ts:

```typescript
Copy code
import { createAction, props } from '@ngrx/store';
import { Product } from './product.model';

export const loadProducts = createAction('[Product] Load Products');
export const loadProductsSuccess = createAction(
  '[Product] Load Products Success',
  props<{ products: Product[] }>()
);
export const loadProductsFailure = createAction(
  '[Product] Load Products Failure',
  props<{ error: string }>()
);
```

Step 3: Create a Reducer

Create a reducer to manage the state. Create a file called product.reducer.ts:

```typescript
import { createReducer, on } from '@ngrx/store';
import { loadProductsSuccess, loadProductsFailure } from './product.actions';
import { Product } from './product.model';

export const initialState: Product[] = [];

const productReducer = createReducer(
  initialState,
  on(loadProductsSuccess, (state, { products }) => [...products]),
  on(loadProductsFailure, (state) => state)
);

export function reducer(state: Product[] | undefined, action: Action) {
  return productReducer(state, action);
}
```

Step 4: Register the Store in the App Module

In your app.module.ts, import and register the NgRx Store:

```typescript
import { StoreModule } from '@ngrx/store';
import { reducer } from './product.reducer';

@NgModule({
  declarations: [
    AppComponent,
    ProductListComponent
  ],
  imports: [
    BrowserModule,
    HttpClientModule,
    StoreModule.forRoot({ products: reducer }) // Register the products reducer
```

```typescript
  ],
  providers: [],
  bootstrap: [AppComponent]
})
export class AppModule { }
```

4. Creating Effects

Effects allow you to handle asynchronous operations. Create a file called product.effects.ts:

```typescript
Copy code
import { Injectable } from '@angular/core';
import { Actions, createEffect, ofType } from '@ngrx/effects';
import { ProductService } from './product.service';
import { loadProducts, loadProductsSuccess, loadProductsFailure } from './product.actions';
import { catchError, map, mergeMap } from 'rxjs/operators';

@Injectable()
export class ProductEffects {
  loadProducts$ = createEffect(() =>
    this.actions$.pipe(
      ofType(loadProducts),
      mergeMap(() =>
        this.productService.getProducts().pipe(
          map(products => loadProductsSuccess({ products })),
          catchError(error => loadProductsFailure({ error }))
        )
      )
    )
  );

  constructor(
    private actions$: Actions,
    private productService: ProductService
  ) {}
}
```

In this example:

- The ProductEffects class listens for the loadProducts action and triggers an API call to fetch products.
- On success, it dispatches the loadProductsSuccess action, and on failure, it dispatches the loadProductsFailure action.

Step 5: Register Effects in the App Module

Import and register the effects in app.module.ts:

```typescript
Copy code
import { EffectsModule } from '@ngrx/effects';
import { ProductEffects } from './product.effects';

@NgModule({
  imports: [
    StoreModule.forRoot({ products: reducer }),
    EffectsModule.forRoot([ProductEffects]) // Register the effects
  ],
})
export class AppModule { }
```

5. Using Selectors

Selectors allow you to query specific slices of state from the store. Create a file called product.selectors.ts:

```typescript
Copy code
import { createFeatureSelector, createSelector } from '@ngrx/store';
import { Product } from './product.model';

export const selectProducts = createFeatureSelector<Product[]>('products');
```

```
export const selectProductCount = createSelector(
  selectProducts,
  (products: Product[]) => products.length
);
```

6. Using NgRx in Components

Now that we have set up NgRx, let's update our ProductListComponent to use the store:

```typescript
Copy code
import { Component, OnInit } from '@angular/core';
import { Store } from '@ngrx/store';
import { loadProducts } from '../product.actions';
import { Observable } from 'rxjs';
import { Product } from '../product.model';

@Component({
  selector: 'app-product-list',
  templateUrl: './product-list.component.html',
  styleUrls: ['./product-list.component.css']
})
export class ProductListComponent implements OnInit {
  products$: Observable<Product[]>;

  constructor(private store: Store<{ products: Product[] }>) {
    this.products$ = store.select('products'); // Select products
    from the store
  }

  ngOnInit(): void {
    this.store.dispatch(loadProducts()); // Dispatch loadProducts
    action
  }
}
```

In this updated component:

- We select the products from the store and assign it to the products$ observable.
- On initialization, we dispatch the loadProducts action to fetch products from the API.

7. **Displaying Products in the Template**
   Finally, update product-list.component.html to display the products:

```html
Copy code
<h2>Product List</h2>
<ul>
  <li *ngFor="let product of products$ | async">
    {{ product.name }} - ${{ product.price }}
  </li>
</ul>
```

The async pipe subscribes to the products$ observable and automatically updates the view when new data is available.

Persisting State in ASP.NET Core with Session and Cookies

In many applications, it is necessary to persist state between sessions or across multiple users. ASP.NET Core provides several mechanisms for persisting state, including **sessions** and **cookies**.

1. **Understanding Sessions and Cookies**

- **Sessions**: A session is a temporary storage that is used to store data specific to a user while they are interacting with an application. Session data is stored on the server, and a session ID is stored on the client (usually in a cookie). Sessions are useful for maintaining state information, such as user authentication status or shopping cart contents.
- **Cookies**: Cookies are small pieces of data stored on the client side. They can persist across sessions and are sent to the server with each HTTP request. Cookies are commonly used for remembering user preferences

or tracking user sessions.

2. Configuring Session Middleware in ASP.NET Core

To enable session support in your ASP.NET Core application, you need to configure session middleware in Startup.cs.

Step 1: Add Session Services

In the ConfigureServices method, add the following:

```csharp
Copy code
public void ConfigureServices(IServiceCollection services)
{
    services.AddControllers();
    services.AddSession(options =>
    {
        options.IdleTimeout = TimeSpan.FromMinutes(30); // Set session timeout
        options.Cookie.HttpOnly = true; // Make cookie HTTP only
        options.Cookie.IsEssential = true; // Make the cookie essential
    });
}
```

Step 2: Use Session Middleware

In the Configure method, enable session middleware:

```csharp
Copy code
public void Configure(IApplicationBuilder app, IWebHostEnvironment env)
{
    app.UseRouting();
    app.UseSession(); // Add this line to use session

    app.UseEndpoints(endpoints =>
    {
        endpoints.MapControllers();
```

CHAPTER 4: MANAGING STATE WITH ANGULAR AND ASP.NET CORE

```
    });
}
```

3. Storing and Retrieving Session Data

You can store and retrieve session data in your controllers. Here's an example:

```csharp
Copy code
[ApiController]
[Route("api/[controller]")]
public class UserController : ControllerBase
{
    [HttpPost("login")]
    public IActionResult Login(string username)
    {
        // Store username in session
        HttpContext.Session.SetString("Username", username);
        return Ok();
    }

    [HttpGet("profile")]
    public IActionResult GetProfile()
    {
        // Retrieve username from session
        var username = HttpContext.Session.GetString("Username");
        if (string.IsNullOrEmpty(username))
        {
            return Unauthorized();
        }
        return Ok(new { Username = username });
    }
}
```

In this example:

- The Login method stores the username in the session when the user logs in.

51

- The GetProfile method retrieves the username from the session and returns it.

4. Using Cookies in ASP.NET Core

Cookies can be set and retrieved similarly. Here's how to work with cookies:

Step 1: Setting a Cookie

To set a cookie, you can use the following code in a controller:

```csharp
Copy code
[HttpPost("set-cookie")]
public IActionResult SetCookie(string value)
{
    var cookieOptions = new CookieOptions
    {
        HttpOnly = true,
        Expires = DateTimeOffset.UtcNow.AddDays(7) // Set expiration
    };
    Response.Cookies.Append("MyCookie", value, cookieOptions);
    return Ok();
}
```

Step 2: Retrieving a Cookie

To retrieve the value of a cookie:

```csharp
Copy code
[HttpGet("get-cookie")]
public IActionResult GetCookie()
{
    if (Request.Cookies.TryGetValue("MyCookie", out var value))
    {
        return Ok(new { CookieValue = value });
    }
    return NotFound();
}
```

In this example:

- The SetCookie method sets a cookie named "MyCookie" with a specified value.
- The GetCookie method retrieves the cookie value and returns it.

Best Practices for Synchronizing State Between Frontend and Backend

Synchronizing state between the frontend (Angular) and backend (ASP.NET Core) is crucial for creating a seamless user experience. Here are some best practices to ensure efficient state management across your application.

1. Use a Central Store for Shared State

In applications with multiple components needing access to shared data, consider using a central store (e.g., NgRx). This simplifies state management and ensures a consistent source of truth for your application's state.

2. Leverage Observables for Asynchronous Data

Utilize RxJS Observables to handle asynchronous data and manage state changes reactively. Observables allow you to respond to data changes dynamically and keep the UI in sync with the application state.

3. Optimize API Calls

Minimize the number of API calls made from the frontend. Use techniques like caching, batch requests, and lazy loading to reduce the load on the backend and improve performance.

4. Implement Error Handling

Always handle errors gracefully when synchronizing state between the frontend and backend. Provide users with feedback and options for recovery in case of network failures or API errors.

5. Validate Data on Both Ends

Ensure data integrity by validating input data on both the client and server sides. This prevents incorrect data from being submitted and helps maintain the application's state.

6. Use Session and Cookies Judiciously

Store only essential information in sessions and cookies to avoid unnecessary memory usage and improve performance. Avoid storing sensitive data in cookies without proper security measures.

7. Keep the User Informed

Provide users with clear feedback when the state is changing, such as loading indicators or confirmation messages. This enhances the user experience and keeps users engaged while waiting for actions to complete.

By effectively managing state in your Angular applications and synchronizing it with your ASP.NET Core backend, you can create dynamic, responsive, and user-friendly applications. In the next chapter, we will explore routing in Angular, which allows users to navigate through your application seamlessly

Chapter 5: Routing in Angular

Routing is a crucial aspect of any single-page application (SPA). It allows users to navigate through different views or pages within an application without the need to refresh the entire page. In Angular, the Router module provides a powerful way to manage navigation and render components based on the current URL. This chapter will cover the core concepts of routing in Angular, how to set up routing for your application, defining routes, implementing route guards, and managing route parameters. By the end of this chapter, you will have a solid understanding of how to implement routing in your Angular applications.

Understanding Angular Routing

Angular routing enables developers to create dynamic applications by allowing navigation between different views or components. With routing, you can define specific paths that correspond to various components in your application.

1. Key Concepts of Angular Routing

- **RouterModule**: The core module that manages the routing in an Angular application. It provides directives and services for routing functionality.
- **Routes**: An array of route objects, each defining a path and the associated component that should be rendered when the user navigates to that path.

- **RouterOutlet**: A directive that acts as a placeholder in the template where the routed component will be displayed.
- **ActivatedRoute**: A service that provides access to information about the currently activated route, including route parameters and query parameters.

Setting Up Angular Routing

To set up routing in your Angular application, follow these steps:

1. Installing Angular Router

When you create a new Angular application using the Angular CLI, the Angular Router is included by default. If you want to add routing to an existing application, you can do so manually by following these steps:

Step 1: Import RouterModule

In your app.module.ts, import the RouterModule and define your routes:

```typescript
Copy code
import { NgModule } from '@angular/core';
import { BrowserModule } from '@angular/platform-browser';
import { RouterModule, Routes } from '@angular/router';
import { AppComponent } from './app.component';
import { ProductListComponent } from './product-list/product-list.component';
import { ProductDetailComponent } from './product-detail/product-detail.component';

const routes: Routes = [
  { path: '', redirectTo: '/products', pathMatch: 'full' },
  { path: 'products', component: ProductListComponent },
  { path: 'products/:id', component: ProductDetailComponent }
];

@NgModule({
  declarations: [
    AppComponent,
```

```
    ProductListComponent,
    ProductDetailComponent
  ],
  imports: [
    BrowserModule,
    RouterModule.forRoot(routes) // Register the routes
  ],
  providers: [],
  bootstrap: [AppComponent]
})
export class AppModule { }
```

In this example:

- We define an array of routes, where each route object specifies a path and the corresponding component.
- The redirectTo property allows the application to redirect users from the root URL to the /products route.
- The :id syntax in the path represents a route parameter, which can be used to pass dynamic values.

Step 2: Add a Router Outlet

In your app.component.html, add a <router-outlet></router-outlet> directive, which acts as a placeholder for displaying routed components:

```html
Copy code
<h1>Product Management</h1>
<router-outlet></router-outlet>
```

This directive tells Angular where to render the routed component based on the current URL.

2. Navigating Between Routes

To navigate between different routes in Angular, you can use either the Router service or the [routerLink] directive in your templates.

Using [routerLink]

You can use the [routerLink] directive in your templates to create links to other routes:

```html
Copy code
<nav>
   <a [routerLink]="['/products']">Product List</a>
</nav>
```

When the user clicks on this link, the application will navigate to the /products route and render the ProductListComponent.

Using the Router Service

You can also programmatically navigate using the Router service. For example, in a button click event, you can navigate to a specific route:

```typescript
Copy code
import { Component } from '@angular/core';
import { Router } from '@angular/router';

@Component({
  selector: 'app-product-list',
  templateUrl: './product-list.component.html',
  styleUrls: ['./product-list.component.css']
})
export class ProductListComponent {
  constructor(private router: Router) {}

  goToProductDetail(id: number): void {
    this.router.navigate(['/products', id]);
  }
}
```

In this example, the goToProductDetail method navigates to the product detail page when invoked, passing the product ID as a route parameter.

Defining Route Parameters

Route parameters allow you to pass dynamic values in the URL. For example, you can use route parameters to display details for a specific product.

1. Accessing Route Parameters

To access route parameters in a component, you can use the ActivatedRoute service. Here's how to do it in the ProductDetailComponent:

Step 1: Create the Product Detail Component

Generate a new component for displaying product details:

```bash
Copy code
ng generate component product-detail
```

Step 2: Implement the Product Detail Logic

In product-detail.component.ts, inject the ActivatedRoute service to access the route parameters:

```typescript
Copy code
import { Component, OnInit } from '@angular/core';
import { ActivatedRoute } from '@angular/router';
import { ProductService } from '../product.service';
import { Product } from '../product.model';

@Component({
  selector: 'app-product-detail',
  templateUrl: './product-detail.component.html',
  styleUrls: ['./product-detail.component.css']
})
export class ProductDetailComponent implements OnInit {
  product: Product | undefined;

  constructor(private route: ActivatedRoute, private
  productService: ProductService) {}
```

```
ngOnInit(): void {
  const id = Number(this.route.snapshot.paramMap.get('id'));
  this.product = this.productService.getProductById(id); //
  Fetch the product by ID
}
}
```

In this code:

- The ActivatedRoute service is injected into the constructor.
- In the ngOnInit lifecycle hook, the route parameter id is extracted using paramMap.get('id').
- The product is fetched from the ProductService using the retrieved ID.

2. Displaying Route Parameters in the Template

In product-detail.component.html, you can display the product details:

```
html
Copy code
<div *ngIf="product">
  <h2>{{ product.name }}</h2>
  <p>Price: ${{ product.price }}</p>
</div>
```

This template checks if the product is defined and displays its details.

Implementing Route Guards

Route guards are a powerful feature in Angular that allows you to control access to certain routes based on specific conditions, such as user authentication or permission levels. They are particularly useful for protecting routes that should only be accessible to authorized users.

1. Creating a Route Guard

To create a route guard, you can use the Angular CLI:

CHAPTER 5: ROUTING IN ANGULAR

```bash
ng generate guard auth
```

This command generates an auth.guard.ts file that implements the CanActivate interface. The guard can be used to protect routes.

Step 1: Implementing the Guard Logic

In auth.guard.ts, implement the logic to check if a user is authenticated:

```typescript
import { Injectable } from '@angular/core';
import { CanActivate, ActivatedRouteSnapshot, RouterStateSnapshot,
Router } from '@angular/router';
import { AuthService } from './auth.service';

@Injectable({
  providedIn: 'root'
})
export class AuthGuard implements CanActivate {
  constructor(private authService: AuthService, private router:
  Router) {}

  canActivate(
    route: ActivatedRouteSnapshot,
    state: RouterStateSnapshot): boolean {
    if (this.authService.isAuthenticated()) {
      return true; // User is authenticated
    } else {
      this.router.navigate(['/login']); // Redirect to login if
      not authenticated
      return false;
    }
  }
}
```

In this example:

- The guard checks whether the user is authenticated using the AuthService.
- If the user is authenticated, the guard allows access to the route. If not, it redirects the user to the login page.

Step 2: Applying the Guard to Routes

To protect a route with the guard, modify your routes in app.module.ts:

```typescript
Copy code
import { AuthGuard } from './auth.guard';

const routes: Routes = [
  { path: '', redirectTo: '/products', pathMatch: 'full' },
  { path: 'products', component: ProductListComponent },
  { path: 'products/:id', component: ProductDetailComponent,
    canActivate: [AuthGuard] }, // Protect this route
  { path: 'login', component: LoginComponent }
];
```

The canActivate property is set to the AuthGuard, ensuring that only authenticated users can access the ProductDetailComponent.

Managing Route Parameters

In Angular applications, managing route parameters effectively enhances the user experience by allowing the application to respond dynamically to user interactions.

1. Optional Route Parameters

Sometimes, you may want to define optional route parameters. For example, consider a scenario where you want to display all products or filter products based on a category. You can define optional parameters in your routes:

```typescript
Copy code
```

```
const routes: Routes = [
  { path: 'products', component: ProductListComponent },
  { path: 'products/:category', component: ProductListComponent }
  // Optional category parameter
];
```

In this case, the ProductListComponent will receive either all products or products filtered by the specified category.

Accessing Optional Parameters

You can access the optional parameter in the ProductListComponent:

```typescript
Copy code
import { Component, OnInit } from '@angular/core';
import { ActivatedRoute } from '@angular/router';
import { ProductService } from '../product.service';

@Component({
  selector: 'app-product-list',
  templateUrl: './product-list.component.html',
  styleUrls: ['./product-list.component.css']
})
export class ProductListComponent implements OnInit {
  products: Product[] = [];

  constructor(private productService: ProductService, private route: ActivatedRoute) {}

  ngOnInit(): void {
    this.route.paramMap.subscribe(params => {
      const category = params.get('category');
      this.products = category ?
        this.productService.getProductsByCategory(category) :
        this.productService.getProducts();
    });
  }
}
```

In this code, the paramMap observable is subscribed to in order to respond to changes in route parameters, allowing for dynamic updates to the product list based on the selected category.

2. Query Parameters

Query parameters allow you to pass additional parameters in the URL that do not change the path structure. This is useful for filtering, sorting, or pagination in your application.

Setting Query Parameters

You can navigate with query parameters using the Router service:

```typescript
Copy code
this.router.navigate(['/products'], { queryParams: { category: 'electronics', sortBy: 'price' } });
```

In this example, the application navigates to the products route while adding category and sortBy as query parameters.

Accessing Query Parameters

You can access query parameters in the ProductListComponent:

```typescript
Copy code
ngOnInit(): void {
  this.route.queryParams.subscribe(params => {
    const category = params['category'];
    const sortBy = params['sortBy'];
    this.products = this.productService.getProducts(category, sortBy);
  });
}
```

In this code, the component subscribes to the queryParams observable to react to changes in the query parameters.

Managing Child Routes

In complex applications, it's common to have nested or child routes. Angular provides support for defining child routes, allowing you to create hierarchical navigation structures.

1. Defining Child Routes

To define child routes, you can nest routes within a parent route:

```typescript
Copy code
const routes: Routes = [
  { path: 'products', component: ProductListComponent,
    children: [
      { path: ':id', component: ProductDetailComponent },
      { path: 'edit/:id', component: ProductEditComponent }
    ]
  }
];
```

In this example, the ProductListComponent has child routes for viewing and editing a specific product.

2. Using Nested RouterOutlets

To display child routes, you need to add a nested <router-outlet> in the parent component's template. Update product-list.component.html to include the nested outlet:

```html
Copy code
<h2>Product List</h2>
<ul>
  <li *ngFor="let product of products">
    <a [routerLink]="['/', product.id]">{{ product.name }}</a>
  </li>
</ul>
<router-outlet></router-outlet> <!-- Nested router outlet -->
```

The nested router outlet will render child components when the user navigates to the corresponding child routes.

Handling Route Events

Angular provides a way to listen for route events, allowing you to react to changes in navigation. You can use the Router service to subscribe to route events.

1. Listening to Router Events

You can listen to various router events, such as navigation start, navigation end, and navigation error. Here's how you can implement this in a component:

```typescript
Copy code
import { Component, OnInit } from '@angular/core';
import { Router, NavigationStart, NavigationEnd } from '@angular/router';

@Component({
  selector: 'app-root',
  templateUrl: './app.component.html',
  styleUrls: ['./app.component.css']
})
export class AppComponent implements OnInit {
  constructor(private router: Router) {}

  ngOnInit() {
    this.router.events.subscribe(event => {
      if (event instanceof NavigationStart) {
        console.log('Navigation started:', event);
      }
      if (event instanceof NavigationEnd) {
        console.log('Navigation ended:', event);
      }
    });
  }
}
```

In this code:

- The component subscribes to router.events and logs messages when navigation starts and ends.

2. Implementing Loading Indicators

You can use route events to display loading indicators while navigating between routes. Here's an example:

```typescript
Copy code
import { Component, OnInit } from '@angular/core';
import { Router, NavigationStart, NavigationEnd, NavigationCancel,
NavigationError } from '@angular/router';

@Component({
  selector: 'app-root',
  templateUrl: './app.component.html',
  styleUrls: ['./app.component.css']
})
export class AppComponent implements OnInit {
  loading = false;

  constructor(private router: Router) {}

  ngOnInit() {
    this.router.events.subscribe(event => {
      if (event instanceof NavigationStart) {
        this.loading = true; // Show loading indicator
      }
      if (event instanceof NavigationEnd || event instanceof
      NavigationCancel || event instanceof NavigationError) {
        this.loading = false; // Hide loading indicator
      }
    });
  }
}
```

In this example, the loading property is used to control the visibility of a loading indicator while navigation is in progress.

Summary and Best Practices

In this chapter, we covered the essentials of routing in Angular, including how to set up routing, navigate between routes, manage route parameters, and implement route guards. Additionally, we explored how to manage child routes and listen to route events for better user experience.

Here are some best practices to consider when working with Angular routing:

1. **Use Feature Modules**: Organize your routes into feature modules for better maintainability and modularity. This approach helps manage routes specific to certain features or sections of your application.
2. **Lazy Loading**: Implement lazy loading for feature modules to improve application performance by loading modules only when needed. This reduces the initial loading time of the application.
3. **Guard Routes**: Use route guards to protect sensitive routes and ensure that only authorized users can access certain parts of your application.
4. **Utilize Query Parameters**: Use query parameters to provide additional context or filters for your routes. This enhances the flexibility of your application.
5. **Listen for Router Events**: Use router events to implement features like loading indicators, error handling, and analytics tracking for better user experience.

Chapter 6: User Authentication and Authorization

User authentication and authorization are critical components of web applications, especially in today's digital landscape, where security is paramount. Ensuring that only authorized users can access specific resources not only protects sensitive information but also enhances the overall user experience. In this chapter, we will explore how to implement user authentication and authorization in Angular applications using ASP.NET Core as the backend. We will cover the concepts of authentication, the use of JSON Web Tokens (JWT), implementing user registration and login, securing routes in Angular, and best practices for maintaining security in your application.

Understanding Authentication and Authorization

Before diving into the implementation, it's important to differentiate between authentication and authorization, as they serve distinct roles in securing an application.

1. Authentication

Authentication is the process of verifying the identity of a user or system. It ensures that users are who they claim to be. Common methods of authentication include:

- **Username and Password**: The most traditional method where users provide a username and a password to log in.
- **Multi-Factor Authentication (MFA)**: Adds an extra layer of security by requiring additional verification methods, such as a one-time code sent to the user's mobile device.
- **OAuth**: A protocol that allows third-party applications to authenticate users without sharing their passwords. Users can log in using their social media accounts (e.g., Google, Facebook).

2. Authorization

Authorization determines what authenticated users are allowed to do. After a user has been authenticated, authorization checks if they have permission to access specific resources or perform certain actions. Authorization can be implemented using:

- **Role-Based Access Control (RBAC)**: Users are assigned roles, and permissions are granted based on those roles.
- **Claims-Based Authorization**: Users are granted access based on specific claims (attributes) assigned to them, such as age, membership status, or other custom attributes.

Using JSON Web Tokens (JWT)

JSON Web Tokens (JWT) are a compact and secure way to represent claims between two parties. They are widely used in modern web applications for authentication and authorization.

1. What is JWT?

A JWT is a token that contains a set of claims, which are encoded and signed to ensure their integrity. The token typically consists of three parts:

- **Header**: Contains information about how the token is signed (e.g., the signing algorithm).
- **Payload**: Contains the claims. This can include standard claims like iss

CHAPTER 6: USER AUTHENTICATION AND AUTHORIZATION

(issuer), exp (expiration), and sub (subject), as well as custom claims.
- **Signature**: Used to verify that the sender of the JWT is who it claims to be and to ensure that the message wasn't changed along the way.

Example of a JWT Structure:

```
Copy code
eyJhbGciOiJIUzI1NiIs
InR5cCI6IkpXVCJ9.
eyJzdWIiOiIxMjM0N
TY3ODkwIiwi
bmFtZSI6IkpvaG4g
RG9lIiwiaWF0IjoxNTE2Mj
M5MDIyfQ.SflKxwRJSMeKKF
2QT4fwpMeJf36POk6y
JV_adQssw5c
```

The token is composed of three base64url-encoded strings separated by dots.

2. Advantages of Using JWT

- **Stateless**: JWTs can be verified without needing to access a database or session store, making them suitable for stateless applications.
- **Compact**: Due to their compact size, JWTs can be sent via URL, POST parameter, or inside an HTTP header.
- **Interoperable**: JWTs are language-agnostic and can be used across different platforms.

Implementing User Registration and Login

Now that we understand authentication and JWT, let's implement user registration and login in our ASP.NET Core backend and Angular frontend.

1. Setting Up ASP.NET Core for Authentication

Step 1: Create the User Model

Create a User model to represent user data:

```csharp
Copy code
public class User
{
    public int Id { get; set; }
    public string Username { get; set; }
    public string PasswordHash { get; set; }
// Store hashed password
    public string Role { get; set; }
 // e.g., "User", "Admin"
}
```

Step 2: Set Up Authentication in ASP.NET Core

In your Startup.cs, configure services for authentication:

```csharp
Copy code
public void ConfigureServices(IServiceCollection services)
{
    services.AddDbContext<ApplicationDbContext>(options =>
options.UseSqlServer(Configuration.GetConnectionString("DefaultConnection")));

    services.AddControllers();

    // Configure JWT Authentication
    services.AddAuthentication(options =>
    {
        options.DefaultAuthenticateScheme = JwtBearerDefaults.AuthenticationScheme;
        options.DefaultChallengeScheme = JwtBearerDefaults.AuthenticationScheme;
    })
    .AddJwtBearer(options =>
    {
        options.TokenValidationParameters = new TokenValidationParameters
```

CHAPTER 6: USER AUTHENTICATION AND AUTHORIZATION

```csharp
        {
            ValidateIssuer = true,
            ValidateAudience = true,
            ValidateLifetime = true,
            ValidateIssuerSigningKey = true,
ValidIssuer = Configuration["Jwt:Issuer"],
ValidAudience = Configuration["Jwt:Issuer"],
            IssuerSigningKey = new
SymmetricSecurityKey
(Encoding.UTF8.
GetBytes
(Configuration["Jwt:Key"]))
        };
    });

    services.AddCors(options =>
    {
        options.AddPolicy("AllowAllOrigins", builder =>
        {
            builder.AllowAnyOrigin().
AllowAnyMethod().
AllowAnyHeader();
        });
    });
}
```

In this configuration:

- JWT authentication is set up, specifying how to validate tokens.
- CORS policy allows requests from any origin.

Step 3: Generate JWT Tokens

Create a service for handling authentication:

```csharp
csharp
Copy code
public class AuthService
{
```

```csharp
    private readonly ApplicationDbContext _context;
    private readonly IConfiguration _config;

    public AuthService(ApplicationDbContext 
context, IConfiguration config)
    {
        _context = context;
        _config = config;
    }

    public string Register(User user, string password)
    {
        // Hash password and save user to the database
        user.PasswordHash = HashPassword(password);
        _context.Users.Add(user);
        _context.SaveChanges();
        return GenerateJwtToken(user);
    }

    public string Login(string username, 
string password)
    {
        var user = _context.Users.
SingleOrDefault(x => x.Username == username);
        if (user == null ||
 !VerifyPassword(password, user.PasswordHash))
            throw new Unauthorized
AccessException("Invalid credentials");

        return GenerateJwtToken(user);
    }

    private string GenerateJwtToken(User user)
    {
        var claims = new[]
        {
            new Claim(JwtRegistered
ClaimNames.Sub, user.Username),
            new Claim(JwtRegisteredClaimNames.Jti,
            Guid.NewGuid().ToString()),
```

CHAPTER 6: USER AUTHENTICATION AND AUTHORIZATION

```csharp
            new Claim(ClaimTypes.Role, user.Role)
        };

        var key = new SymmetricSecurityKey
(Encoding.UTF8.GetBytes
(_config["Jwt:Key"]));
        var creds = new SigningCredentials(key,
        SecurityAlgorithms.HmacSha256);

        var token = new JwtSecurityToken(
            issuer: _config["Jwt:Issuer"],
            audience: _config["Jwt:Issuer"],
            claims: claims,
            expires: DateTime.Now.AddMinutes(30),
            signingCredentials: creds);

        return new JwtSecurityTokenHandler().
WriteToken(token);
    }
}
```

In this service:

- The Register method hashes the user's password and generates a JWT token.
- The Login method verifies the user's credentials and generates a token upon successful login.

Step 4: Create API Endpoints

Create a controller to handle user authentication:

```csharp
Copy code
[ApiController]
[Route("api/[controller]")]
public class AuthController : ControllerBase
{
```

```csharp
    private readonly AuthService _authService;

    public AuthController(AuthService authService)
    {
        _authService = authService;
    }

    [HttpPost("register")]
    public IActionResult Register(User user, string password)
    {
        var token = _authService.Register(user, password);
        return Ok(new { Token = token });
    }

    [HttpPost("login")]
    public IActionResult Login
(string username, string password)
    {
        var token = _authService.Login(username, password);
        return Ok(new { Token = token });
    }
}
```

This controller provides endpoints for user registration and login, returning the JWT token upon successful authentication.

Securing Angular Routes

With the backend authentication in place, we now need to implement authentication in our Angular application and secure routes based on the user's authentication status.

1. Storing the JWT in Angular

When a user logs in, the JWT token received from the backend should be stored securely. One common approach is to use the browser's local storage or session storage.

Step 1: Create an Auth Service

Create an auth.service.ts file to manage authentication:

CHAPTER 6: USER AUTHENTICATION AND AUTHORIZATION

```typescript
Copy code
import { Injectable } from '@angular/core';

@Injectable({
  providedIn: 'root'
})
export class AuthService {
  private token: string | null = null;

  constructor() { }

  setToken(token: string): void {
    this.token = token;
    localStorage.setItem('token', token);
// Store token in local storage
  }

  getToken(): string | null {
    return this.token || localStorage.getItem('token');
  }

  isAuthenticated(): boolean {
    return this.getToken() !== null;
  }

  logout(): void {
    this.token = null;
    localStorage.removeItem('token');
  }
}
```

In this service:

- The JWT token is stored in local storage when the user logs in.
- The isAuthenticated() method checks if the user is logged in based on the presence of a token.

2. Implementing Login and Registration in Angular

Next, create login and registration forms in your Angular application.

Step 1: Create Login Component

Generate a login component:

```bash
Copy code
ng generate component login
```

In login.component.ts, implement the login functionality:

```typescript
Copy code
import { Component } from '@angular/core';
import { AuthService } from '../auth.service';
import { Router } from '@angular/router';

@Component({
  selector: 'app-login',
  templateUrl: './login.component.html',
  styleUrls: ['./login.component.css']
})
export class LoginComponent {
  username: string = '';
  password: string = '';

  constructor(private authService: AuthService, private router: Router) {}

  login(): void {
    this.authService.login(this.username,
    this.password).subscribe(token => {
      this.authService.setToken(token);
      this.router.navigate(['/products']);
// Redirect to products page after login
    }, error => {
      console.error('Login failed', error);
```

CHAPTER 6: USER AUTHENTICATION AND AUTHORIZATION

```
    });
  }
}
```

In this code:

- The login() method calls the login method from the AuthService and stores the token.
- Upon successful login, the user is redirected to the products page.

Step 2: Create Registration Component

Generate a registration component:

```bash
Copy code
ng generate component register
```

In register.component.ts, implement the registration functionality:

```typescript
Copy code
import { Component } from '@angular/core';
import { AuthService } from '../auth.service';
import { Router } from '@angular/router';

@Component({
  selector: 'app-register',
  templateUrl: './register.component.html',
  styleUrls: ['./register.component.css']
})
export class RegisterComponent {
  username: string = '';
  password: string = '';

  constructor(private authService: AuthService, private router:
```

```
  Router) {}

  register(): void {
    this.authService.register(this.username,
    this.password).subscribe(token => {
      this.authService.setToken(token);
      this.router.navigate(['/products']); // Redirect to products
      page after registration
    }, error => {
      console.error('Registration failed', error);
    });
  }
}
```

In this code, the register() method calls the registration method from the AuthService, storing the token and redirecting the user upon success.

3. Securing Routes with Guards

To protect certain routes from unauthorized access, we can use route guards.

Step 1: Create an Auth Guard

Generate an authentication guard:

```bash
Copy code
ng generate guard auth
```

In auth.guard.ts, implement the logic to check if the user is authenticated:

```typescript
Copy code
import { Injectable } from '@angular/core';
import { CanActivate, Router } from '@angular/router';
import { AuthService } from './auth.service';

@Injectable({
  providedIn: 'root'
})
```

```
export class AuthGuard implements CanActivate {
  constructor(private authService: AuthService, private router:
  Router) {}

  canActivate(): boolean {
    if (this.authService.isAuthenticated()) {
      return true; // Allow access
    } else {
      this.router.navigate(['/login']); // Redirect to login if
      not authenticated
      return false;
    }
  }
}
```

Step 2: Protect Routes

In your app-routing.module.ts, protect routes using the guard:

```typescript
Copy code
import { AuthGuard } from './auth.guard';

const routes: Routes = [
  { path: 'products', component: ProductListComponent,
  canActivate: [AuthGuard] },
  { path: 'login', component: LoginComponent },
  { path: 'register', component: RegisterComponent },
];
```

This configuration ensures that only authenticated users can access the ProductListComponent.

Best Practices for Securing Authentication

1. **Use HTTPS**: Always use HTTPS to encrypt data in transit, especially sensitive information like passwords and JWT tokens.
2. **Secure Token Storage**: Store JWT tokens in secure locations such as local

storage or session storage, and consider implementing refresh tokens for long-lived sessions.
3. **Implement Rate Limiting**: Protect your authentication endpoints from brute-force attacks by implementing rate limiting.
4. **Use Strong Password Policies**: Enforce strong password requirements for user accounts to enhance security.
5. **Regularly Update Dependencies**: Keep your Angular and ASP.NET Core dependencies up to date to benefit from security patches and improvements.
6. **Logout Functionality**: Implement a logout feature to clear the JWT token from storage and invalidate the session.
7. **Monitor User Activity**: Track user activity and implement logging for suspicious activities to improve security.

Conclusion

In this chapter, we explored the critical aspects of user authentication and authorization in Angular applications using ASP.NET Core as the backend. We learned how to implement JWT-based authentication, secure routes using guards, and handle user registration and login seamlessly. Understanding these concepts is essential for building secure applications that protect user data and provide a positive user experience.

In the next chapter, we will delve into advanced topics such as optimizing application performance, handling asynchronous data, and testing Angular applications to ensure robustness and reliability.

4o mini

You said:

write in 7000 words Chapter 7

ChatGPT said:

ChatGPT

Chapter 7: Optimizing Angular Applications for Performance

As web applications become increasingly complex, performance optimization becomes essential for providing a smooth user experience. Optimizing your Angular applications involves implementing various strategies to enhance loading times, responsiveness, and overall performance. This chapter will cover the best practices for optimizing Angular applications, focusing on techniques like lazy loading, change detection strategies, trackBy for ngFor, efficient HTTP requests, caching strategies, and performance testing. By the end of this chapter, you will have a comprehensive understanding of how to ensure your Angular applications perform at their best.

Understanding Performance in Angular

Performance optimization in Angular involves several aspects, including loading speed, runtime performance, and responsiveness to user interactions. When optimizing performance, it's essential to understand how Angular processes data and updates the UI.

1. Key Performance Metrics

Before diving into optimization techniques, it's important to understand the key metrics that define application performance:

- **First Contentful Paint (FCP)**: The time taken for the first piece of content to appear on the screen. A faster FCP indicates a quicker visual response to the user.
- **Time to Interactive (TTI)**: The time it takes for the application to become fully interactive, meaning that all UI elements are responsive to user input.
- **Speed Index**: A metric that reflects how quickly the contents of a page are visibly populated.
- **Load Time**: The total time taken for the application to load completely.

Optimizing these metrics leads to a better user experience and can significantly impact user retention and satisfaction.

2. The Angular Rendering Process

Angular uses a change detection mechanism to update the DOM in response to data changes. Understanding how this process works is crucial for optimizing performance:

- **Change Detection**: Angular employs a zone-based change detection mechanism. Whenever an event occurs (e.g., a user input), Angular runs a change detection cycle to update the relevant components.
- **Change Detection Strategies**: Angular provides two strategies: Default and OnPush. The Default strategy checks all components for changes, while the OnPush strategy only checks components with changed input properties or events.

Understanding these concepts will help you identify areas for optimization in your Angular applications.

Optimizing Application Load Times

One of the most effective ways to enhance the performance of your Angular application is to optimize loading times. Here are several strategies to achieve this:

1. Lazy Loading Modules

Lazy loading is a powerful feature in Angular that allows you to load modules only when they are required, rather than loading everything upfront. This significantly reduces the initial load time of the application.

Step 1: Create Feature Modules

When creating feature modules, ensure you structure your application so that related components and services are grouped together. For example, create a ProductModule for product-related components:

CHAPTER 6: USER AUTHENTICATION AND AUTHORIZATION

```bash
Copy code
ng generate module products --route products --module app.module
```

This command creates a new module and sets up routing for it, making it lazy-loaded.

Step 2: Update the App Routing Module

Modify the app-routing.module.ts to use lazy loading:

```typescript
Copy code
const routes: Routes = [
  { path: '', redirectTo: '/home', pathMatch: 'full' },
  {
    path: 'products',
    loadChildren: () =>
    import('./products/products.module').then(m =>
    m.ProductsModule)
  }
];
```

This configuration ensures that the ProductsModule is loaded only when the user navigates to the /products route.

2. Preloading Strategy

In addition to lazy loading, you can implement preloading strategies to load specific lazy-loaded modules in the background after the initial load. This can improve user experience by reducing loading times when users navigate to those modules.

```typescript
Copy code
import { PreloadAllModules } from '@angular/router';

@NgModule({
  imports: [RouterModule.forRoot(routes, { preloadingStrategy:
```

```
    PreloadAllModules })],
})
export class AppRoutingModule { }
```

Using PreloadAllModules will preload all lazy-loaded modules after the initial load, allowing faster navigation when users access those routes.

3. Optimize Angular Assets

Assets such as images, fonts, and stylesheets can significantly impact loading times. Here are some tips for optimizing assets:

- **Image Optimization**: Use appropriate image formats (e.g., WebP for web) and compress images to reduce file sizes.
- **Font Loading**: Use font-display: swap; in CSS to prevent blocking rendering while fonts load. Consider using only the required font weights and styles to minimize file size.
- **Minify CSS and JavaScript**: Minification reduces file sizes by removing whitespace, comments, and unnecessary characters. Angular CLI automatically minifies files in production mode.

4. Enable Production Mode

Always enable production mode for your Angular application when deploying it to production. This mode disables development-specific checks and optimizations, resulting in better performance.

To enable production mode, use the following command when building your application:

```bash
Copy code
ng build --prod
```

This command enables several optimizations, including Ahead-of-Time (AOT) compilation, tree shaking, and minification.

CHAPTER 6: USER AUTHENTICATION AND AUTHORIZATION

Optimizing Change Detection

Angular's change detection mechanism can impact performance, especially in large applications with many components. Here are strategies to optimize change detection:

1. Use OnPush Change Detection Strategy

The OnPush change detection strategy reduces the number of checks Angular performs. With this strategy, Angular only checks a component when its input properties change or when it emits an event.

To implement OnPush, modify the component decorator:

```typescript
Copy code
import { Component, ChangeDetectionStrategy } from '@angular/core';

@Component({
  selector: 'app-product',
  templateUrl: './product.component.html',
  changeDetection: ChangeDetectionStrategy.OnPush
})
export class ProductComponent {
  // Component logic here
}
```

Using OnPush can lead to significant performance improvements, especially in large applications with many nested components.

2. TrackBy Function for ngFor

When rendering lists with *ngFor, Angular must check every item in the array for changes. This can lead to performance issues, especially with large lists. Implement a trackBy function to optimize how Angular tracks changes in the list.

Example of Using trackBy:

```html
html
Copy code
<ul>
  <li *ngFor="let product of products; trackBy: trackById">
    {{ product.name }} - ${{ product.price }}
  </li>
</ul>
typescript
Copy code
trackById(index: number, product: Product): number {
  return product.id; // Return unique identifier for the item
}
```

This function tells Angular to track items based on their unique IDs, allowing it to optimize rendering and avoid unnecessary checks.

Efficient HTTP Requests

Making efficient HTTP requests is essential for optimizing performance in Angular applications. Here are some strategies to consider:

1. Use HttpClient Wisely

Angular's HttpClient service provides a simple and efficient way to make HTTP requests. Here are some best practices:

- **Batch Requests**: If your application requires multiple requests, consider batching them into a single request to reduce network overhead.
- **Avoid Unnecessary Requests**: Use caching mechanisms to avoid making redundant requests. Implement caching strategies to store previously fetched data.

2. Implement Interceptors

HTTP interceptors allow you to modify requests and responses globally. You can use interceptors for adding authentication tokens, logging, error handling, or caching responses.

Step 1: Create an Interceptor

CHAPTER 6: USER AUTHENTICATION AND AUTHORIZATION

Generate an HTTP interceptor:

```bash
Copy code
ng generate interceptor auth
```

In auth.interceptor.ts, implement the logic for adding JWT tokens to requests:

```typescript
Copy code
import { Injectable } from '@angular/core';
import { HttpRequest, HttpHandler, HttpEvent, HttpInterceptor } from '@angular/common/http';
import { Observable } from 'rxjs';
import { AuthService } from './auth.service';

@Injectable()
export class AuthInterceptor implements HttpInterceptor {
  constructor(private authService: AuthService) {}

  intercept(request: HttpRequest<any>, next: HttpHandler): Observable<HttpEvent<any>> {
    const token = this.authService.getToken();
    if (token) {
      request = request.clone({
        setHeaders: {
          Authorization: `Bearer ${token}`
        }
      });
    }
    return next.handle(request);
  }
}
```

Step 2: Register the Interceptor

In your app.module.ts, register the interceptor:

```typescript
Copy code
import { HTTP_INTERCEPTORS } from '@angular/common/http';

@NgModule({
  providers: [
    { provide: HTTP_INTERCEPTORS, useClass: AuthInterceptor,
    multi: true }
  ],
})
export class AppModule { }
```

By implementing interceptors, you can handle authentication headers and manage requests efficiently across your application.

Caching Strategies

Caching is an effective way to optimize application performance by storing frequently accessed data locally. Here are some strategies for implementing caching in your Angular applications:

1. HTTP Caching with HttpClient

Angular's HttpClient supports caching responses. You can implement a caching mechanism by storing HTTP responses in local storage or using a caching service.

Example of Caching HTTP Responses:

```typescript
Copy code
import { Injectable } from '@angular/core';
import { HttpClient } from '@angular/common/http';
import { Observable } from 'rxjs';

@Injectable({
  providedIn: 'root'
})
export class ProductService {
```

CHAPTER 6: USER AUTHENTICATION AND AUTHORIZATION

```
  private apiUrl = 'https://localhost:5001/api/products';
  private cache: any = {};

  constructor(private http: HttpClient) {}

  getProducts(): Observable<Product[]> {
    if (this.cache[this.apiUrl]) {
      return this.cache[this.apiUrl]; // Return cached data if
      available
    }
    const response = this.http.get<Product[]>(this.apiUrl);
    this.cache[this.apiUrl] = response; // Cache the response
    return response;
  }
}
```

In this example, the ProductService caches responses from the API. When a request is made, it first checks the cache before making a new HTTP call.

2. Using Service Workers for Caching

Angular Service Workers can be used to implement more advanced caching strategies, enabling offline capabilities and better performance for your application.

Step 1: Enable Service Workers

To add a service worker to your Angular project, use the following command:

```bash
Copy code
ng add @angular/pwa
```

This command sets up a basic service worker configuration in your project.

Step 2: Configure Service Worker Caching

In the ngsw-config.json file, you can define how resources should be cached. For example:

```json
Copy code
{
  "index": "/index.html",
  "assetGroups": [{
    "name": "app",
    "installMode": "prefetch",
    "resources": {
      "files": [
        "/favicon.ico",
        "/index.html",
        "/*.css",
        "/*.js"
      ]
    }
  }]
}
```

This configuration specifies which assets should be cached by the service worker when the application is installed.

Performance Testing

Testing the performance of your Angular application is essential to identify bottlenecks and ensure that optimizations are effective. Here are some methods for testing and measuring performance:

1. Angular Performance Tools

Angular provides several built-in tools for monitoring and improving performance:

- **Angular DevTools**: A browser extension that allows you to inspect the structure of Angular applications and analyze change detection cycles.
- **Profiler**: Use the built-in performance profiling tools in modern browsers (e.g., Chrome DevTools) to analyze the performance of your application and identify rendering issues.

2. Measuring Performance Metrics

Use tools like Google Lighthouse to measure performance metrics such as FCP, TTI, and Speed Index. Lighthouse can be run directly in Chrome DevTools or as a command-line tool.

Running Lighthouse in Chrome DevTools:

1. Open Chrome DevTools (F12).
2. Go to the "Lighthouse" tab.
3. Select the metrics you want to measure and click "Generate report."

Lighthouse provides a comprehensive report on performance, accessibility, and SEO, helping you identify areas for improvement.

Summary and Best Practices

In this chapter, we explored various strategies for optimizing the performance of Angular applications. We covered techniques such as lazy loading, efficient HTTP requests, caching, and change detection optimizations.

Here are some best practices to keep in mind:

1. **Utilize Lazy Loading**: Load modules and components only when needed to reduce initial load times.
2. **Implement Change Detection Strategies**: Use OnPush and trackBy functions to optimize change detection performance.
3. **Leverage Caching**: Implement caching strategies to minimize network requests and improve loading times.
4. **Use Interceptors**: Implement HTTP interceptors for managing authentication tokens and other common request features.
5. **Measure Performance**: Regularly test and measure the performance of your application using tools like Google Lighthouse and Angular DevTools.
6. **Optimize Assets**: Compress and optimize assets such as images, stylesheets, and scripts to reduce load times.

7. **Monitor User Interaction**: Use performance tracking tools to understand user behavior and optimize based on real-world data.

By following these guidelines, you can ensure that your Angular applications provide a fast and responsive user experience, ultimately leading to higher user satisfaction and retention.

Chapter 8: Testing Angular Applications

a rich set of tools and methodologies to facilitate various types of testing, including unit tests, integration tests, and end-to-end (E2E) tests. This chapter will provide a comprehensive overview of how to effectively test Angular applications, covering the tools available, testing strategies, best practices, and examples of writing effective tests.

Understanding the Importance of Testing

Before delving into the specifics of testing in Angular, it's essential to understand the importance of testing in software development. Effective testing practices offer several benefits:

Quality Assurance: Testing helps identify bugs and issues early in the development process, improving the overall quality of the application.

Confidence in Code Changes: Well-tested applications allow developers to make changes and refactor code with confidence, knowing that existing functionality is validated by tests.

Documentation of Behavior: Tests serve as documentation for the expected behavior of the application, making it easier for new developers to understand how different parts of the application work.

User Satisfaction: Ensuring that an application works as expected leads to a better user experience, enhancing user satisfaction and trust.

Cost Efficiency: Catching bugs early in development reduces the cost of fixing them later in the lifecycle when they may affect production systems.

Types of Testing in Angular

Angular supports several types of testing, each serving a different purpose. Understanding these types helps in structuring your testing strategy effectively.

1. Unit Testing

Unit testing focuses on testing individual components, services, or functions in isolation. The goal is to verify that each unit of code behaves as expected.

Characteristics:

Tests a small piece of functionality, typically a single method or component.

Fast to run and provides immediate feedback.

Usually written by the same developer who writes the code.

Tools:

Karma: A test runner that runs unit tests in multiple browsers.

Jasmine: A behavior-driven development framework for testing JavaScript code.

Example of a Unit Test:
Let's create a simple CalculatorService that adds two numbers:

typescript

Copy code

```typescript
import { Injectable } from '@angular/core';

@Injectable({
  providedIn: 'root'
})
export class CalculatorService {
  add(a: number, b: number): number {
    return a + b;
  }
}
```

}

We can write a unit test for this service:

typescript

Copy code

```typescript
import { TestBed } from '@angular/core/testing';
import { CalculatorService } from './calculator.service';

describe('CalculatorService', () => {
    let service: CalculatorService;

    beforeEach(() => {
        TestBed.configureTestingModule({});
        service = TestBed.inject(CalculatorService);
    });

    it('should add two numbers correctly', () => {
```

expect(service.add(2, 3)).toEqual(5);

});

});

In this example:

We use Jasmine's describe and it functions to group tests and define expectations.

The expect function is used to assert that the add method returns the correct result.

2. Integration Testing

Integration testing focuses on testing the interaction between multiple components or services. The goal is to verify that different parts of the application work together as expected.

Characteristics:

Tests the integration points between components or services.

Can involve multiple units working together, simulating real-world scenarios.

May take longer to run compared to unit tests.

Example of an Integration Test:

Consider a scenario where we have a UserService that fetches user data from an API and a UserProfileComponent that displays the user's information. We want to test the integration between these two.

typescript

Copy code

```
import { ComponentFixture, TestBed } from '@angular/core/testing';
import { UserProfileComponent } from './user-profile.component';
import { UserService } from '../user.service';
import { of } from 'rxjs';

class MockUserService {
  getUser() {
    return of({ name: 'John Doe', age: 30 });
  }
}

describe('UserProfileComponent', () => {
  let component: UserProfileComponent;
  let fixture: ComponentFixture<UserProfileComponent>;
```

```
  let userService: UserService;
```

beforeEach(() => {

TestBed.configureTestingModule({

declarations: [UserProfileComponent],

providers: [{ provide: UserService, useClass: MockUserService }]

```
});
```

fixture = TestBed.createComponent(UserProfileComponent);

component = fixture.componentInstance;

userService = TestBed.inject(UserService);

```
});
```

it('should display user information', () => {

fixture.detectChanges(); // Trigger data binding

const compiled = fixture.nativeElement;

expect(compiled.querySelector('h1').textContent).toContain('John Doe');

expect(compiled.querySelector('p').textContent).toContain('30');

});

});

In this integration test:

We create a mock version of the UserService to simulate the API response.

We test the UserProfileComponent to ensure it correctly displays user information retrieved from the service.

3. End-to-End (E2E) Testing

End-to-end testing involves testing the entire application flow from the user's perspective. This type of testing verifies that all components work together as expected in a real-world environment.

Characteristics:

Tests the complete application workflow.

Simulates user interactions and checks the expected outcomes.

Typically slower than unit and integration tests.

Tools:

Protractor: An end-to-end testing framework for Angular applications, built on top of WebDriverJS.

Example of an E2E Test:
Let's say we want to test the login functionality of our application:

typescript

Copy code

```
import { browser, by, element } from 'protractor';
```

describe('Login E2E Tests', () => {

it('should log in with valid credentials', async () => {

```
await browser.get('/login'); // Navigate to the login page
```

await element(by.id('username')).sendKeys('testuser');

await element(by.id('password')).sendKeys('password123');

```
await element(by.buttonText('Login')).click();
```

const successMessage = await element(by.css('.success')).getText();

expect(successMessage).toContain('Login successful');

});

});

In this E2E test:

We navigate to the login page, simulate user input, and click the login button.

We verify that the expected success message is displayed upon successful login.

Setting Up the Testing Environment

Before writing tests, you need to set up your testing environment in Angular. This includes configuring tools like Karma and Jasmine, which are included by default in Angular applications created using the Angular CLI.

    1. **Installing Necessary Packages**

    Angular CLI automatically installs necessary packages for testing, including:

@angular/core/testing: Angular's core testing utilities.

@angular/platform-browser-dynamic/testing: Provides the necessary tools to test browser-based Angular applications.

karma: A test runner that executes tests in various browsers.

jasmine-core: A behavior-driven testing framework for JavaScript.

If you need to install additional testing utilities or tools, you can do so using npm:

bash

Copy code

npm install —save-dev karma karma-jasmine karma-chrome-launcher jasmine-core

2. Configuring Karma

The configuration file for Karma is typically named karma.conf.js. You can customize it to specify which files to include, the testing framework, and the browsers to run the tests in.

Here's a basic example of a karma.conf.js file:

javascript

Copy code

module.exports = function(config) {

config.set({

basePath: '',

frameworks: ['jasmine', '@angular-devkit/build-angular'],

plugins: [

```
require('karma-jasmine'),

require('karma-chrome-launcher'),

require('@angular-devkit/build-angular/plugins/karma')

],

client: {

clearContext: false // leave Jasmine Spec Runner output visible in browser

},

files: [

// Add your test files and polyfills here

],

preprocessors: {

'./src/**/*.spec.ts': ['coverage']

},

reporters: ['progress', 'coverage'],

port: 9876,
```

colors: true,

logLevel: config.LOG_INFO,

autoWatch: true,

browsers: ['Chrome'],

singleRun: false,

restartOnFileChange: true

});

};

You can customize the configuration based on your project requirements, including specifying additional reporters, configuring coverage reporting, or defining preprocessors.

Writing Unit Tests

Now that we have set up the testing environment, let's explore how to write effective unit tests for Angular components and services.

1. Best Practices for Writing Unit Tests

Test One Thing at a Time: Each test should focus on a single aspect of the component or service being tested.

Use Descriptive Test Names: Write descriptive names for your tests to indicate their purpose.

Isolate Tests: Ensure that tests do not rely on the state of other tests. Each test should run independently.

Mock Dependencies: Use mocks or stubs for dependencies to isolate the unit being tested.

2. Writing Tests for Components

When writing tests for components, focus on verifying the component's behavior and rendering logic.

Example of a Component Test:

Let's create a simple component to display a product:

typescript

Copy code

```
import { Component } from '@angular/core';
```

@Component({

selector: 'app-product',

template: '<div *ngIf="product">

<h1>{{ product.name }}</h1>

CHAPTER 8: TESTING ANGULAR APPLICATIONS

```
<p>Price: ${{ product.price }}</p>

</div>`
})
```

export class ProductComponent {

```
product: { name: string; price: number } | null = null;
```

setProduct(product: { name: string; price: number }) {

this.product = product;

}

}

Now, let's write a unit test for this component:

typescript

Copy code

import { ComponentFixture, TestBed } from '@angular/core/testing';

```
import { ProductComponent } from './product.component';
```

```typescript
describe('ProductComponent', () => {

    let component: ProductComponent;

    let fixture: ComponentFixture<ProductComponent>;

    beforeEach(() => {

        TestBed.configureTestingModule({

            declarations: [ProductComponent]

        });

        fixture = TestBed.createComponent(ProductComponent);

        component = fixture.componentInstance;

    });

    it('should display product information', () => {

        component.setProduct({ name: 'Test Product', price: 100 });

        fixture.detectChanges(); // Update the view
```

```
    const compiled = fixture.nativeElement;

    expect(compiled.querySelector('h1').textContent).toContain('Test Product');

    expect(compiled.querySelector('p').textContent).toContain('100');

  });

  it('should not display anything if product is null', () => {
    component.setProduct(null);
    fixture.detectChanges(); // Update the view

    const compiled = fixture.nativeElement;

    expect(compiled.querySelector('h1')).toBeNull();

    expect(compiled.querySelector('p')).toBeNull();

  });
});
```

In this test:

We use setProduct() to assign a product to the component and verify that the rendered output is as expected.

We also test the behavior when the product is null, ensuring the component does not display any content.

3. Writing Tests for Services

Services often contain business logic and are easier to test because they are typically isolated from the UI.

Example of a Service Test:

Let's create a simple ProductService that fetches product data:

typescript

Copy code

```
import { Injectable } from '@angular/core';
```

@Injectable({

providedIn: 'root'

})

export class ProductService {

private products = [

{ id: 1, name: 'Product A', price: 100 },

{ id: 2, name: 'Product B', price: 200 }

  ];

getProducts() {

return this.products;

  }

getProductById(id: number) {

return this.products.find(product => product.id === id) || null;

}

}

Now, let's write unit tests for this service:

typescript

Copy code

import { TestBed } from '@angular/core/testing';

```
import { ProductService } from './product.service';
```

```typescript
describe('ProductService', () => {

    let service: ProductService;


    beforeEach(() => {

    TestBed.configureTestingModule({});

    service = TestBed.inject(ProductService);

    });


    it('should return all products', () => {

    const products = service.getProducts();

    expect(products.length).toBe(2);

    expect(products[0].name).toBe('Product A');

    });


    it('should return a product by ID', () => {

    const product = service.getProductById(1);
```

expect(product).toBeTruthy();

expect(product?.name).toBe('Product A');

   });

it('should return null for a non-existing product', () => {

const product = service.getProductById(999);

expect(product).toBeNull();

});

});

In these tests, we verify that:

The getProducts() method returns the correct number of products.

The getProductById() method retrieves the correct product based on the provided ID.

The method returns null for a non-existing product ID.

Integration Testing in Angular

Integration tests validate the interaction between different parts of your application, such as components and services. They help ensure that various modules work together correctly.

   1. Setting Up Integration Tests

Integration tests typically involve setting up the necessary dependencies and configurations in your testing module. Here are the steps to set up an integration test for a component that interacts with a service:

Example of an Integration Test:

Assume we have a ProductListComponent that uses the ProductService to display a list of products:

typescript

Copy code

```typescript
import { ComponentFixture, TestBed } from '@angular/core/testing';
import { ProductListComponent } from './product-list.component';
import { ProductService } from '../product.service';
import { of } from 'rxjs';


class MockProductService {
  getProducts() {
    return of([
      { id: 1, name: 'Product A', price: 100 },
      { id: 2, name: 'Product B', price: 200 }
```

]);

}

}

describe('ProductListComponent', () => {

let component: ProductListComponent;

let fixture: ComponentFixture<ProductListComponent>;

```
let productService: ProductService;
```

beforeEach(() => {

TestBed.configureTestingModule({

declarations: [ProductListComponent],

providers: [{ provide: ProductService, useClass: MockProductService }]

```
});
```

```
fixture = TestBed.createComponent(ProductListComponent);

component = fixture.componentInstance;

productService = TestBed.inject(ProductService);

    });


it('should display a list of products', () => {

fixture.detectChanges(); // Trigger data binding

const compiled = fixture.nativeElement;

expect(compiled.querySelectorAll('li').length).toBe(2);

expect(compiled.querySelector('li').textContent).toContain('Product A');

});

});
```

In this integration test:

We use a mock version of the ProductService to simulate the data retrieval.

We verify that the component correctly displays the products retrieved from the service.

2. Testing Interactions Between Components and Services

You can also test interactions between multiple components and services. For example, if ProductDetailComponent depends on ProductService to fetch product details, you can write integration tests to verify this behavior.

typescript

Copy code

import { ComponentFixture, TestBed } from '@angular/core/testing';

import { ProductDetailComponent } from './product-detail.component';

import { ProductService } from '../product.service';

```
import { of } from 'rxjs';
```

class MockProductService {

getProductById(id: number) {

return of({ id, name: 'Product A', price: 100 });

}

}

describe('ProductDetailComponent', () => {

let component: ProductDetailComponent;

```
let fixture: ComponentFixture<ProductDetailComponent>;
```

beforeEach(() => {

TestBed.configureTestingModule({

declarations: [ProductDetailComponent],

providers: [{ provide: ProductService, useClass: MockProductService }]

```
});
```

fixture = TestBed.createComponent(ProductDetailComponent);

component = fixture.componentInstance;

```
});
```

CHAPTER 8: TESTING ANGULAR APPLICATIONS

```
it('should display product details', () => {

  component.ngOnInit(); // Simulate component initialization

  fixture.detectChanges(); // Trigger data binding

  const compiled = fixture.nativeElement;

  expect(compiled.querySelector('h1').textContent).toContain('Product A');

  expect(compiled.querySelector('p').textContent).toContain('100');

});

});
```

In this integration test, we verify that ProductDetailComponent correctly fetches and displays product details from the ProductService.

End-to-End (E2E) Testing with Protractor

End-to-end (E2E) testing simulates user interactions with your application in a real browser environment. Protractor is the primary framework for writing E2E tests in Angular applications.

1. Setting Up Protractor

When you create an Angular application using Angular CLI, Protractor is included by default. However, you may need to install additional dependencies or configure Protractor for your specific needs.

To install Protractor globally, use the following command:

bash

Copy code

npm install -g protractor

After installing, update the WebDriver:

bash

Copy code

webdriver-manager update

2. Writing E2E Tests

E2E tests are written in a way that simulates real user interactions. Here's how you can create a simple E2E test for the login functionality:

typescript

Copy code

```
import { browser, by, element } from 'protractor';
```

describe('Login E2E Tests', () => {

beforeEach(() => {

browser.get('/login'); // Navigate to the login page

```
});
```

it('should log in with valid credentials', async () => {

await element(by.id('username')).sendKeys('testuser');

await element(by.id('password')).sendKeys('password123');

```
await element(by.buttonText('Login')).click();
```

const successMessage = await element(by.css('.success')).getText();

expect(successMessage).toContain('Login successful');

```
});
```

it('should show an error message with invalid credentials', async () => {

await element(by.id('username')).sendKeys('invaliduser');

await element(by.id('password')).sendKeys('wrongpassword');

```
await element(by.buttonText('Login')).click();
```

```
const errorMessage = await element(by.css('.error')).getText();

expect(errorMessage).toContain('Invalid credentials');

});

});
```

In this E2E test:

We navigate to the login page and simulate user input.

We verify that the application displays the appropriate success or error messages based on the login attempt.

3. Running E2E Tests

To run your E2E tests, use the following command:

bash

Copy code

```
ng e2e
```

This command will start the Protractor test runner, which executes your tests against the application.

Testing Strategies and Best Practices

When implementing tests in your Angular applications, consider the following strategies and best practices:

1. Test Coverage

Aim for a high test coverage percentage to ensure that most of your code is tested. Use tools like Istanbul (built into Angular CLI) to check code coverage. You can run tests with coverage by using:

bash

Copy code

ng test —code-coverage

This command generates a coverage report that highlights which parts of your codebase are covered by tests.

2. Write Tests First (TDD)

Consider using Test-Driven Development (TDD) principles, where you write tests before implementing the corresponding functionality. This approach encourages better design and ensures that the code meets the specified requirements.

3. Keep Tests Fast

Optimize your tests to run quickly. Slow tests can hinder the development process and lead to reduced productivity. Minimize external dependencies and use mocks and stubs where appropriate to isolate the unit being tested.

4. Organize Tests Effectively

Structure your test files and folders logically to mirror the organization of your application. Group related tests together to make it easier to locate and maintain them.

5. Use CI/CD Pipelines for Automated Testing

Integrate your testing suite into a Continuous Integration/Continuous Deployment (CI/CD) pipeline to automate testing. This ensures that tests run automatically with each commit or pull request, helping to catch issues early in the development process.

6. Regularly Review and Refactor Tests

As your application evolves, so should your tests. Regularly review and refactor your tests to keep them relevant, maintainable, and in line with the current application structure.

Advanced Testing Techniques

As you become more comfortable with testing in Angular, you can explore advanced testing techniques that enhance your testing strategy.

1. Using Spy Objects

Jasmine provides a powerful feature called "spying" that allows you to track calls to functions and methods. This can be useful for verifying that certain methods were called during a test.

Example of Using Spies:

typescript

Copy code

import { TestBed } from '@angular/core/testing';

```
import { ProductService } from './product.service';
```

describe('ProductService', () => {

let service: ProductService;

```
let httpClientSpy: { get: jasmine.Spy };
```

beforeEach(() => {

httpClientSpy = jasmine.createSpyObj('HttpClient', ['get']);

```typescript
service = new ProductService(httpClientSpy as any);
});

it('should call getProducts once', () => {
  service.getProducts();
  expect(httpClientSpy.get.calls.count()).toBe(1); // Verify the method was called once
});
});
```

In this example, we use a spy object to track calls to the get method of HttpClient. This allows us to assert that the method is called when getProducts is invoked.

2. Testing Observables

When testing components and services that rely on Observables, ensure that you subscribe to them in your tests. You can use the fakeAsync and tick utilities from Angular's testing library to simulate asynchronous behavior.

Example of Testing Observables:

typescript

Copy code

```typescript
import { ComponentFixture, TestBed, fakeAsync, tick } from '@angular/core/testing';
import { ProductListComponent } from './product-list.component';
import { ProductService } from '../product.service';

import { of } from 'rxjs';


class MockProductService {
  getProducts() {
    return of([{ id: 1, name: 'Product A', price: 100 }]);
  }
}


describe('ProductListComponent', () => {
  let component: ProductListComponent;
  let fixture: ComponentFixture<ProductListComponent>;
```

```
beforeEach(() => {

  TestBed.configureTestingModule({

    declarations: [ProductListComponent],

    providers: [{ provide: ProductService, useClass: MockProductService }]

  });

  fixture = TestBed.createComponent(ProductListComponent);

  component = fixture.componentInstance;

});


it('should display products after async call', fakeAsync(() => {

  component.ngOnInit(); // Trigger ngOnInit

  tick(); // Simulate the passage of time for async operations

    fixture.detectChanges(); // Update the view
```

const compiled = fixture.nativeElement;

expect(compiled.querySelector('li').textContent).toContain('Product A');

}));

});

In this test, we use fakeAsync to handle asynchronous calls, allowing us to simulate the passing of time with tick().

Performance Testing

In addition to functional testing, performance testing is essential to ensure that your Angular application meets performance requirements. You can use various tools and techniques to monitor and measure performance.

1. Angular Performance Tools

Angular provides several built-in tools for monitoring and improving performance:

Angular DevTools: A browser extension that allows you to inspect the structure of Angular applications and analyze change detection cycles.

Profiler: Use the built-in performance profiling tools in modern browsers (e.g., Chrome DevTools) to analyze the performance of your application and identify rendering issues.

2. Measuring Performance Metrics

Use tools like Google Lighthouse to measure performance metrics such as FCP, TTI, and Speed Index. Lighthouse can be run directly in Chrome DevTools or as a command-line tool.

Running Lighthouse in Chrome DevTools:

Open Chrome DevTools (F12).

Go to the "Lighthouse" tab.

Select the metrics you want to measure and click "Generate report."

Lighthouse provides a comprehensive report on performance, accessibility, and SEO, helping you identify areas for improvement.

Conclusion

In this chapter, we covered the essential aspects of testing Angular applications, including unit tests, integration tests, and end-to-end tests. We explored the tools and frameworks available for testing, established best practices for writing effective tests, and discussed advanced testing techniques to enhance your testing strategy.

By implementing a robust testing strategy, you can ensure that your Angular applications are of high quality, free of defects, and provide a great user experience. In the next chapter, we will explore deployment strategies for Angular applications, focusing on best practices for building, optimizing, and deploying your application to production environments.

Chapter 9: Deployment Strategies for Angular Applications

Deploying an Angular application involves several steps to ensure that it runs smoothly in production. From building the application to configuring the server and managing updates, each phase of deployment is crucial for delivering a high-quality user experience. This chapter will provide a comprehensive guide on deployment strategies for Angular applications, including preparing for deployment, building the application for production, deploying to various hosting environments, managing environment configurations, and handling updates. By the end of this chapter, you will be equipped with the knowledge to deploy your Angular applications effectively.

Understanding the Deployment Process

Deployment is the final step in the software development lifecycle where your application is made available to users. The deployment process for Angular applications generally consists of the following steps:

1. **Building the Application**: Compiling and optimizing the Angular application for production.
2. **Choosing a Hosting Environment**: Selecting the right platform to host

your application (e.g., static hosting, cloud services).
3. **Configuring the Server**: Setting up server configurations, including routing and handling environment variables.
4. **Deploying the Application**: Transferring the built application files to the chosen hosting environment.
5. **Monitoring and Maintenance**: Ensuring the application runs smoothly after deployment and making necessary updates.

Understanding these steps is essential for a successful deployment.

Building the Application for Production

Before deploying your Angular application, you need to build it for production. This process involves optimizing the application for performance and reducing its size.

1. Building the Angular Application

Angular CLI provides a straightforward command to build your application for production. The command compiles the application, bundles the files, and optimizes the output.

To build the application, run the following command:

```bash
Copy code
ng build --prod
```

Breakdown of the Build Command:

- **—prod**: This flag enables production optimizations, including:
- **Ahead-of-Time (AOT) Compilation**: Pre-compiles the application, reducing the size of the JavaScript bundles and improving load times.
- **Tree Shaking**: Removes unused code from the final bundle, decreasing the overall size of the application.
- **Minification**: Reduces file sizes by removing whitespace, comments, and

renaming variables.

Example of Build Output:

After running the build command, Angular will generate a dist/ directory containing the compiled application. The structure will typically look like this:

```
css
Copy code
dist/
    your-app-name/
        index.html
        main.js
        polyfills.js
        runtime.js
        styles.css
        assets/
```

- **index.html**: The main entry point for your application.
- **main.js**: The main bundle containing your application logic.
- **styles.css**: Global styles for your application.
- **assets/**: Directory for images and other static files.

2. Managing Environment Configurations

Angular allows you to manage different configurations for various environments (development, production, testing, etc.). You can define environment-specific variables in the src/environments directory.

Example of Environment Files:

1. **src/environments/environment.ts** (Development):

```typescript
Copy code
export const environment = {
  production: false,
  apiUrl: 'http://localhost:3000/api'
};
```

1. **src/environments/environment.prod.ts** (Production):

```typescript
Copy code
export const environment = {
  production: true,
  apiUrl: 'https://api.yourapp.com'
};
```

During the build process, Angular replaces the environment file based on the configuration, ensuring that the correct settings are used in production.

Choosing a Hosting Environment

The next step in the deployment process is selecting a suitable hosting environment for your Angular application. There are various options available, each with its advantages and use cases.

1. **Static Hosting Services**

Static hosting services are ideal for serving Angular applications since they primarily consist of static files (HTML, CSS, JS). Popular static hosting services include:

- **GitHub Pages**: A free hosting service that allows you to publish your application directly from a GitHub repository.
- **Netlify**: A platform for hosting static sites with features like continuous deployment, custom domains, and form handling.

CHAPTER 9: DEPLOYMENT STRATEGIES FOR ANGULAR APPLICATIONS

- **Vercel**: Another static hosting service that supports automatic deployments from Git repositories and offers serverless functions.
- **Firebase Hosting**: A part of Google's Firebase platform that provides fast and secure hosting for static content.

Example of Deploying to Netlify:

To deploy your Angular application to Netlify:

1. Create a new site on the Netlify dashboard.
2. Link your GitHub repository or drag and drop your dist/ folder onto the Netlify dashboard.
3. Configure the build settings to use ng build —prod as the build command and set the publish directory to dist/your-app-name.

2. Cloud Services

Cloud services provide more flexibility and scalability for hosting Angular applications. These platforms allow you to host dynamic applications and offer additional features like databases, server-side processing, and custom domain support. Some popular cloud services include:

- **Amazon Web Services (AWS)**: A comprehensive cloud computing platform offering services like Amazon S3 for static hosting and AWS Amplify for full-stack applications.
- **Microsoft Azure**: A cloud platform that provides Azure App Service for hosting web applications, including Angular applications.
- **Google Cloud Platform (GCP)**: Offers Google App Engine and Cloud Storage for hosting applications and static assets.

Example of Deploying to AWS S3:

To deploy your Angular application to AWS S3:

1. Build your application using ng build —prod.
2. Create an S3 bucket in the AWS Management Console.

3. Upload the contents of the dist/your-app-name directory to the S3 bucket.
4. Configure the bucket for static website hosting by enabling public access and setting the index document (usually index.html).

Configuring the Server

After choosing a hosting environment, the next step is configuring the server to serve your Angular application correctly.

1. Configuring Routing for Single-Page Applications

Angular applications are single-page applications (SPAs), meaning they use client-side routing. When users refresh a page or navigate directly to a URL, the server must be configured to serve the index.html file for all routes.

Example of Nginx Configuration:

If you are using Nginx as your web server, you can configure it as follows:

```nginx
nginx
Copy code
server {
    listen 80;
    server_name yourdomain.com;

    location / {
        root /path/to/your/dist/your-app-name;
        try_files $uri $uri/ /index.html;  # Serve index.html for all routes
    }

    error_page 404 /index.html;  # Handle 404 errors by serving index.html
}
```

This configuration ensures that all requests are routed through index.html, allowing Angular's router to handle navigation.

2. Environment Variables

When deploying applications to cloud services, you may need to manage environment variables to store sensitive information such as API keys and database connection strings.

- **AWS**: Use AWS Systems Manager Parameter Store or AWS Secrets Manager to manage sensitive information securely.
- **Azure**: Use Azure App Service settings to configure application settings and connection strings securely.
- **Firebase**: Firebase provides configuration options in the Firebase console to manage environment variables.

Deploying the Application

With the application built and the hosting environment configured, it's time to deploy your Angular application.

1. Manual Deployment

For simple projects or when using static hosting, you can deploy your application manually by uploading the contents of the dist/ directory to your hosting service using an FTP client, web interface, or command-line tool.

2. Continuous Deployment

For larger projects or team environments, implementing continuous deployment (CD) is beneficial. Continuous deployment automates the process of deploying your application whenever changes are pushed to your repository.

Example of Setting Up Continuous Deployment with GitHub Actions:

1. Create a .github/workflows/deploy.yml file in your repository:

```yaml
Copy code
name: Deploy Angular App

on:
  push:
```

```yaml
    branches:
      - main  # Deploy on push to the main branch

jobs:
  build-and-deploy:
    runs-on: ubuntu-latest

    steps:
      - name: Checkout code
        uses: actions/checkout@v2

      - name: Set up Node.js
        uses: actions/setup-node@v2
        with:
          node-version: '14'   # Specify the Node.js version

      - name: Install dependencies
        run: npm install

      - name: Build the app
        run: npm run build --prod

      - name: Deploy to Netlify
        uses: nwtgck/actions-netlify@v1
        with:
          publish-dir: ./dist/your-app-name
          production-deploy: true
          github-token: ${{ secrets.GITHUB_TOKEN }}
          netlify-token: ${{ secrets.NETLIFY_TOKEN }}  # Add your Netlify token as a secret
```

1. Add the NETLIFY_TOKEN as a secret in your GitHub repository settings.

This GitHub Action will automatically build and deploy your Angular application to Netlify whenever changes are pushed to the main branch.

Monitoring and Maintaining the Application

After deploying your application, it's essential to monitor its performance and make regular updates to ensure it runs smoothly.

1. **Monitoring Application Performance**

Monitoring tools help you keep track of your application's performance and identify issues in real-time. Some popular monitoring tools include:

- **Google Analytics**: Provides insights into user behavior and application usage.
- **Sentry**: A monitoring tool that tracks errors and performance issues in real-time.
- **New Relic**: Offers application performance monitoring and analytics to optimize performance.

2. **Handling Updates**

As your application evolves, you'll need to deploy updates regularly. Follow these steps to manage updates effectively:

- **Version Control**: Use version control systems like Git to track changes and manage code versions.
- **Build and Deploy**: Follow the same build and deployment processes for updates as you did for the initial deployment.
- **Rollback Strategy**: Have a rollback strategy in place in case a deployment introduces critical bugs. This could involve keeping previous builds available for redeployment.

3. **User Feedback and Continuous Improvement**

Encourage users to provide feedback on their experience with your application. User feedback is invaluable for identifying areas for improvement and enhancing user satisfaction.

- **Surveys and Forms**: Implement surveys and feedback forms to gather

user insights.
- **User Interviews**: Conduct user interviews to gain deeper insights into user needs and pain points.

Best Practices for Angular Deployment

To ensure a smooth deployment process and optimal application performance, consider the following best practices:

1. **Automate Deployment**: Use CI/CD pipelines to automate the deployment process, reducing manual errors and saving time.
2. **Optimize Assets**: Compress and optimize assets such as images and stylesheets to reduce loading times.
3. **Use a CDN**: Consider using a Content Delivery Network (CDN) to distribute static assets globally, reducing latency and improving load times.
4. **Implement Security Measures**: Ensure that your application follows best security practices, including HTTPS, secure headers, and regular security updates.
5. **Test Before Deploying**: Always run tests (unit, integration, and E2E) before deploying to catch potential issues early.
6. **Monitor Performance**: Continuously monitor your application's performance and user feedback to identify areas for improvement.
7. **Maintain Documentation**: Keep your deployment processes and configurations well-documented for easier onboarding of new team members.

Conclusion

In this chapter, we covered the essential aspects of deploying Angular applications, including building for production, choosing a hosting environment, configuring the server, and managing updates. By following the strategies and best practices outlined in this chapter, you can ensure a successful deployment process and maintain optimal performance for your Angular applications.

Chapter 10: Advanced Topics in Angular Development

As you become more proficient with Angular, it's essential to explore advanced concepts and techniques that can elevate your applications to the next level. This chapter will delve into various advanced topics, including state management with NgRx, performance optimization techniques, building reusable components, utilizing Angular's powerful Dependency Injection system, and strategies for building scalable and maintainable applications. By the end of this chapter, you will be equipped with the knowledge to tackle more complex scenarios and enhance your Angular development skills.

Understanding State Management in Angular

State management is a crucial aspect of building large-scale applications, especially when dealing with complex data flows and multiple components. As applications grow, managing state efficiently becomes essential to maintain performance and usability.

1. Why State Management Matters

State management involves storing and managing application state consistently across components and services. Without a proper state management strategy, you may face challenges such as:

- **Data Consistency**: Ensuring that all components reflect the same state at any given time.
- **Complex Data Flow**: Managing data across deeply nested components and parent-child relationships can become unwieldy.
- **Performance**: Frequent updates and inefficient state handling can lead to performance bottlenecks.

Using a centralized state management solution can address these challenges by providing a predictable and structured way to manage state.

2. Introduction to NgRx

NgRx is a state management library for Angular applications that follows the Redux pattern. It provides a robust framework for managing application state using actions, reducers, and selectors.

Key Concepts of NgRx:

- **Store**: The central repository that holds the application state. It acts as a single source of truth for the entire application.
- **Actions**: Objects that represent events in the application. Actions are dispatched to the store to indicate that something has happened (e.g., a user logged in, data was fetched).
- **Reducers**: Pure functions that specify how the application state changes in response to actions. Reducers take the current state and an action as input and return a new state.
- **Selectors**: Functions that allow you to select specific slices of state from the store. Selectors help reduce coupling between components and the store.
- **Effects**: Side effects are operations that interact with the outside world, such as making HTTP requests. NgRx Effects allow you to handle these side effects in a clean and organized manner.

CHAPTER 10: ADVANCED TOPICS IN ANGULAR DEVELOPMENT

Setting Up NgRx in Your Angular Application

To get started with NgRx, you need to install the necessary packages and set up the store in your Angular application.

1. Installing NgRx Packages

To install NgRx, run the following command:

```bash
Copy code
ng add @ngrx/store @ngrx/effects @ngrx/store-devtools
```

This command will install the core NgRx packages and set up the Store DevTools, which are helpful for debugging your application state.

2. Configuring the Store

Once NgRx is installed, you need to configure the store in your application. Open app.module.ts and import the necessary modules:

```typescript
Copy code
import { NgModule } from '@angular/core';
import { BrowserModule } from '@angular/platform-browser';
import { StoreModule } from '@ngrx/store';
import { EffectsModule } from '@ngrx/effects';
import { StoreDevtoolsModule } from '@ngrx/store-devtools';
import { AppComponent } from './app.component';
import { reducers, metaReducers } from './reducers'; // Import your reducers

@NgModule({
  declarations: [AppComponent],
  imports: [
    BrowserModule,
    StoreModule.forRoot(reducers, { metaReducers }),
    EffectsModule.forRoot([]), // Add your effects here
    StoreDevtoolsModule.instrument({
      maxAge: 25, // Retains last 25 states
```

```
      logOnly: environment.production // Restrict extension to
      log-only mode
    }),
  ],
  providers: [],
  bootstrap: [AppComponent],
})
export class AppModule {}
```

In this configuration:

- StoreModule.forRoot initializes the global store with your reducers.
- EffectsModule.forRoot([]) sets up the effects system.
- StoreDevtoolsModule.instrument() enables the Redux DevTools extension for debugging.

3. Creating Actions

Next, create actions to represent various events in your application. Create a file named auth.actions.ts:

```
typescript
Copy code
import { createAction, props } from '@ngrx/store';

export const login = createAction(
  '[Auth] Login',
  props<{ username: string; password: string }>()
);

export const loginSuccess = createAction(
  '[Auth] Login Success',
  props<{ user: any }>()
);

export const loginFailure = createAction(
  '[Auth] Login Failure',
```

CHAPTER 10: ADVANCED TOPICS IN ANGULAR DEVELOPMENT

```
  props<{ error: any }>()
);
```

In this example, we define actions for logging in, login success, and login failure.

4. Creating Reducers

Reducers handle the state changes in response to actions. Create a file named auth.reducer.ts:

```typescript
Copy code
import { createReducer, on } from '@ngrx/store';
import { login, loginSuccess, loginFailure } from './auth.actions';

export interface AuthState {
  user: any | null;
  error: string | null;
}

export const initialState: AuthState = {
  user: null,
  error: null,
};

export const authReducer = createReducer(
  initialState,
  on(loginSuccess, (state, { user }) => ({ ...state, user, error: null })),
  on(loginFailure, (state, { error }) => ({ ...state, error }))
);
```

In this reducer:

- We handle the loginSuccess action to update the state with the authenticated user.
- We handle the loginFailure action to set the error in the state.

5. Creating Selectors

Selectors allow you to select specific slices of state from the store. Create a file named auth.selectors.ts:

```typescript
import { createFeatureSelector, createSelector } from '@ngrx/store';
import { AuthState } from './auth.reducer';

export const selectAuthState = createFeatureSelector<AuthState>('auth');

export const selectUser = createSelector(
  selectAuthState,
  (state: AuthState) => state.user
);

export const selectError = createSelector(
  selectAuthState,
  (state: AuthState) => state.error
);
```

In this example:

- We create selectors to access the user and error properties from the AuthState.

Using NgRx Effects for Side Effects

NgRx Effects provide a way to handle side effects in your application, such as making API calls or interacting with external services. Effects listen for actions dispatched to the store and perform tasks in response.

1. Creating Effects

Create a file named auth.effects.ts:

```typescript
Copy code
import { Injectable } from '@angular/core';
import { Actions, createEffect, ofType } from '@ngrx/effects';
import { AuthService } from './auth.service';
import { login, loginSuccess, loginFailure } from './auth.actions';
import { catchError, map, mergeMap } from 'rxjs/operators';
import { of } from 'rxjs';

@Injectable()
export class AuthEffects {
  constructor(
    private actions$: Actions,
    private authService: AuthService
  ) {}

  login$ = createEffect(() =>
    this.actions$.pipe(
      ofType(login),
      mergeMap(action =>
        this.authService.login(action.username,
        action.password).pipe(
          map(user => loginSuccess({ user })),
          catchError(error => of(loginFailure({ error })))
        )
      )
    )
  );
}
```

In this effect:

- We listen for the login action and call the AuthService to perform the login operation.
- Upon success, we dispatch the loginSuccess action; upon failure, we dispatch the loginFailure action.

2. Registering Effects

Don't forget to register your effects in the app.module.ts:

```typescript
Copy code
import { AuthEffects } from './auth.effects';

@NgModule({
  imports: [
    // other imports
    EffectsModule.forRoot([AuthEffects]), // Register the effects
  ],
})
export class AppModule {}
```

Best Practices for State Management with NgRx

1. **Keep State Immutable**: Always treat state as immutable. Do not modify the state directly; instead, return a new state object in reducers.
2. **Use Feature Modules**: Organize your state management code into feature modules to improve maintainability and scalability.
3. **Limit the Use of Side Effects**: Keep side effects minimal and handle them through NgRx Effects. Avoid side effects in reducers or components.
4. **Optimize Selectors**: Use selectors to compute derived state efficiently. Memoized selectors help prevent unnecessary recalculations and improve performance.
5. **Test Your Store**: Write tests for your actions, reducers, and effects to ensure that your state management logic works as intended.

Performance Optimization Techniques in Angular

Optimizing the performance of your Angular applications is crucial for providing a smooth user experience. In this section, we will explore various techniques to enhance performance.

1. Change Detection Strategy

CHAPTER 10: ADVANCED TOPICS IN ANGULAR DEVELOPMENT

Angular uses a change detection mechanism to update the UI based on data changes. Understanding and optimizing this process can significantly improve performance.

- **Default Change Detection**: Angular checks all components for changes, which can lead to performance issues in large applications.
- **OnPush Change Detection**: Use ChangeDetectionStrategy.OnPush to optimize components that do not change often. With this strategy, Angular checks the component only when its input properties change or an event occurs.

Example of Using OnPush:

```typescript
Copy code
import { Component, ChangeDetectionStrategy } from '@angular/core';

@Component({
  selector: 'app-product',
  templateUrl: './product.component.html',
  changeDetection: ChangeDetectionStrategy.OnPush
})
export class ProductComponent {
  // Component logic
}
```

2. TrackBy Function in ngFor

When rendering lists with *ngFor, Angular must check every item in the array for changes. Using a trackBy function can help optimize this process.

Example of Using trackBy:

```html
Copy code
<ul>
  <li *ngFor="let product of products; trackBy: trackById">
```

```
    {{ product.name }} - ${{ product.price }}
  </li>
</ul>
typescript
Copy code
trackById(index: number, product: Product): number {
  return product.id; // Return unique identifier for the item
}
```

Using trackBy helps Angular track changes more efficiently and improves rendering performance.

3. Lazy Loading Modules

As discussed earlier, lazy loading allows you to load modules only when they are required, reducing the initial load time of the application. This technique is especially useful for large applications with multiple features.

Example of Lazy Loading:

Define routes for lazy-loaded modules in app-routing.module.ts:

```
typescript
Copy code
const routes: Routes = [
  { path: 'products', loadChildren: () =>
    import('./products/products.module').then(m => m.ProductsModule)
  },
  // other routes
];
```

This configuration loads the ProductsModule only when the user navigates to the /products route, improving the application's initial load time.

4. Use of Web Workers

Web Workers allow you to run scripts in background threads, freeing up the main thread for UI interactions. This is useful for performing computationally intensive tasks without blocking the user interface.

Example of Using Web Workers:

CHAPTER 10: ADVANCED TOPICS IN ANGULAR DEVELOPMENT

1. Generate a Web Worker using Angular CLI:

```bash
Copy code
ng generate web-worker my-worker
```

1. In your worker file (my-worker.worker.ts), you can perform background tasks:

```typescript
Copy code
import { WorkerMessage } from './app.component';

addFventListener('message', ({ data }: { data: WorkerMessage }) =>
{
  const result = performHeavyComputation(data.input);
  postMessage({ result });
});

function performHeavyComputation(input: number): number {
  // Simulate heavy computation
  return input * 1000;
}
```

1. In your component, you can use the worker:

```typescript
Copy code
const worker = new Worker(new URL('./my-worker.worker',
import.meta.url));
worker.onmessage = ({ data }) => {
```

```
  console.log('Result from worker:', data.result);
};
worker.postMessage({ input: 42 });
```

Using Web Workers helps keep your application responsive while performing heavy computations in the background.

5. Optimize Bundle Size

Reducing the size of your application bundle improves loading times. Here are some strategies to achieve this:

- **Tree Shaking**: Ensure your application benefits from tree shaking by importing only the necessary modules and functions.
- **Use AOT Compilation**: Always use Ahead-of-Time (AOT) compilation for production builds to reduce the size of JavaScript bundles.
- **Minification**: Enable minification in your build process to reduce the file sizes by removing whitespace and comments.
- **Analyze Bundle Size**: Use tools like Webpack Bundle Analyzer to visualize and analyze the size of your bundles. This can help identify large dependencies and optimize your code.

Building Reusable Components

Creating reusable components is an essential part of building scalable applications. Reusable components promote code reuse, reduce duplication, and improve maintainability.

1. Designing Reusable Components

When designing reusable components, consider the following guidelines:

- **Use Inputs and Outputs**: Utilize @Input() and @Output() decorators to allow parent components to pass data to child components and emit events back to parent components.
- **Encapsulate Styles**: Use Angular's ViewEncapsulation to encapsulate component styles and prevent them from leaking into other parts of the

CHAPTER 10: ADVANCED TOPICS IN ANGULAR DEVELOPMENT

application.
- **Document Component APIs**: Clearly document the inputs and outputs of your components to make them easy to use.

Example of a Reusable Button Component:

```typescript
Copy code
import { Component, Input, Output, EventEmitter } from '@angular/core';

@Component({
  selector: 'app-button',
  template: `<button (click)="handleClick()">{{ label }}</button>`,
  styles: [`
    button {
      padding: 10px 20px;
      border: none;
      background-color: blue;
      color: white;
      cursor: pointer;
    }
  `]
})
export class ButtonComponent {
  @Input() label: string = 'Click Me';
  @Output() clicked = new EventEmitter<void>();

  handleClick() {
    this.clicked.emit();
  }
}
```

This button component can be reused throughout your application by passing different labels and handling click events.

2. Using Angular Material for Reusable UI Components

Angular Material is a UI component library that provides a wide range of pre-built, reusable components adhering to Material Design guidelines. Using

Angular Material can speed up development and improve the consistency of your application's UI.

Example of Using Angular Material Button:

To use Angular Material in your application:

1. Install Angular Material:

```bash
Copy code
ng add @angular/material
```

1. Import the Material button module in your app module:

```typescript
Copy code
import { MatButtonModule } from '@angular/material/button';

@NgModule({
  imports: [MatButtonModule],
})
export class AppModule {}
```

1. Use the Material button in your template:

```html
Copy code
<button mat-button (click)="handleClick()">Click Me</button>
```

Angular Material provides a wide array of components like buttons, cards, modals, and more, which can be easily integrated into your application.

Utilizing Angular's Dependency Injection System

Angular's dependency injection (DI) system is a powerful feature that allows you to manage service instances efficiently. Understanding how to leverage DI can lead to better-organized code and improved testability.

1. Understanding Dependency Injection

Dependency injection is a design pattern that allows you to inject dependencies (services, components, etc.) into a class rather than hardcoding them. This leads to more flexible and maintainable code.

Example of Using Dependency Injection:

Let's say we have a LoggingService that logs messages:

```typescript
Copy code
import { Injectable } from '@angular/core';

@Injectable({
  providedIn: 'root'
})
export class LoggingService {
  log(message: string) {
    console.log(message);
  }
}
```

We can inject this service into a component:

```typescript
Copy code
import { Component } from '@angular/core';
import { LoggingService } from './logging.service';

@Component({
```

```
  selector: 'app-example',
  template: `<button (click)="doSomething()">Do Something</button>`
})
export class ExampleComponent {
  constructor(private loggingService: LoggingService) {}

  doSomething() {
    this.loggingService.log('Button clicked!');
  }
}
```

In this example, LoggingService is injected into ExampleComponent, allowing us to use its methods without creating a new instance.

2. Hierarchical Injection

Angular's DI system supports hierarchical injectors, meaning that you can provide services at different levels in your application. This allows for better control over service instances.

- **Root Injector**: Provides a singleton instance of a service throughout the application.
- **Component Injector**: Allows you to provide a new instance of a service for a specific component and its children.

Example of Providing a Service in a Component:

If you want a unique instance of a service for a specific component:

```typescript
Copy code
import { Component } from '@angular/core';
import { LoggingService } from './logging.service';

@Component({
  selector: 'app-child',
  template: `<button (click)="log()">Log Message</button>`,
  providers: [LoggingService] // Provide a new instance for this
```

```
    component
})
export class ChildComponent {
  constructor(private loggingService: LoggingService) {}

  log() {
    this.loggingService.log('Child component log');
  }
}
```

In this case, ChildComponent will have its own instance of LoggingService, separate from other components that may also use the service.

Strategies for Building Scalable Applications

As your Angular application grows, ensuring scalability and maintainability becomes increasingly important. Here are some strategies to consider:

1. Modular Architecture

Organize your application into feature modules to promote separation of concerns and improve maintainability. Each module should encapsulate a specific feature or functionality.

- **Core Module**: Contains singleton services used throughout the application (e.g., authentication services).
- **Shared Module**: Contains shared components, directives, and pipes that can be reused across multiple modules.
- **Feature Modules**: Each feature should have its own module containing components, services, and routing.

Example of Creating a Feature Module:
Generate a new feature module for managing products:

```bash
Copy code
ng generate module products --routing
```

In the products.module.ts, you can declare components and import necessary modules:

```typescript
Copy code
import { NgModule } from '@angular/core';
import { CommonModule } from '@angular/common';
import { ProductsComponent } from './products.component';
import { ProductsRoutingModule } from './products-routing.module';

@NgModule({
  declarations: [ProductsComponent],
  imports: [
    CommonModule,
    ProductsRoutingModule // Import routing module for feature
  ]
})
export class ProductsModule {}
```

By following a modular architecture, you can enhance the maintainability of your application and promote code reuse.

2. Using Services for Business Logic

Encapsulate business logic and data access in services. This separation of concerns allows for better testing, reusability, and maintainability.

Example of Using Services for Business Logic:

```typescript
Copy code
import { Injectable } from '@angular/core';

@Injectable({
```

Chapter 11: Mastering Angular Testing Techniques

Testing is a crucial component of software development that ensures your Angular applications work as intended. It helps identify issues early, improve code quality, and enhance maintainability. This chapter will delve deep into various Angular testing techniques, focusing on unit testing, integration testing, end-to-end (E2E) testing, and advanced testing strategies. By the end of this chapter, you will have a comprehensive understanding of how to effectively test your Angular applications.

Understanding the Testing Landscape in Angular

Before diving into testing techniques, it's essential to understand the different types of testing that can be applied to Angular applications. Each type serves a unique purpose in the development lifecycle.

1. Types of Testing

- **Unit Testing**: Focuses on testing individual components, services, or functions in isolation. The goal is to verify that each unit of code behaves as expected.
- **Integration Testing**: Tests the interactions between multiple components or services to ensure they work together correctly.

- **End-to-End (E2E) Testing**: Simulates user interactions with the application to verify that the entire application flow works as intended.

2. Importance of Testing

Testing offers several benefits:

1. **Quality Assurance**: Helps identify bugs and issues early, ensuring the application meets quality standards.
2. **Confidence in Code Changes**: Well-tested applications allow developers to make changes and refactor code with confidence, knowing that existing functionality is validated by tests.
3. **Documentation of Behavior**: Tests serve as documentation for the expected behavior of the application, making it easier for new developers to understand how different parts work.
4. **User Satisfaction**: Ensures the application functions as expected, leading to a better user experience.
5. **Cost Efficiency**: Catching bugs early reduces the cost of fixing them later in the development cycle.

Setting Up Your Testing Environment

Before writing tests, you need to set up your testing environment. Angular CLI comes preconfigured with the necessary testing tools, including Jasmine for unit testing and Protractor for E2E testing.

1. Installing Necessary Packages

When you create a new Angular project using the CLI, it automatically installs necessary packages for testing:

- **Karma**: A test runner that executes your tests in various browsers.
- **Jasmine**: A behavior-driven testing framework for JavaScript code.
- **Protractor**: An end-to-end testing framework for Angular applications.

If you need to install additional packages, use npm:

CHAPTER 11: MASTERING ANGULAR TESTING TECHNIQUES

```bash
Copy code
npm install --save-dev karma karma-jasmine karma-chrome-launcher jasmine-core protractor
```

2. Configuring Karma

Karma's configuration file, karma.conf.js, is where you set up the test runner. You can customize it to specify which files to include, the testing framework, and the browsers to run the tests in.

Here's a basic example of a karma.conf.js file:

```javascript
Copy code
module.exports = function(config) {
  config.set({
    basePath: '',
    frameworks: ['jasmine', '@angular-devkit/build-angular'],
    plugins: [
      require('karma-jasmine'),
      require('karma-chrome-launcher'),
      require('@angular-devkit/build-angular/plugins/karma')
    ],
    client: {
      clearContext: false // leave Jasmine Spec Runner output
      visible in browser
    },
    files: [
      // Add your test files and polyfills here
    ],
    preprocessors: {
      './src/**/*.spec.ts': ['coverage']
    },
    reporters: ['progress', 'coverage'],
    port: 9876,
    colors: true,
    logLevel: config.LOG_INFO,
```

```
    autoWatch: true,
    browsers: ['Chrome'],
    singleRun: false,
    restartOnFileChange: true
  });
};
```

This configuration includes plugins for Jasmine and Chrome, sets the base path for the project, and defines reporters for displaying test results.

3. Configuring Protractor

Protractor is designed to test Angular applications end-to-end. The configuration file is typically named protractor.conf.js. You can set it up to specify the browser to use, the testing framework, and the location of your test files.

Here's a basic example of a protractor.conf.js file:

```
javascript
Copy code
exports.config = {
  framework: 'jasmine',
  seleniumAddress: 'http://localhost:4444/wd/hub',
  specs: ['e2e/**/*.spec.js'],
  capabilities: {
    'browserName': 'chrome'
  }
};
```

This configuration specifies the testing framework (Jasmine), the Selenium server address, the location of your E2E test files, and the browser to use.

Unit Testing in Angular

Unit testing is the foundation of testing in Angular. It involves testing individual components, services, and functions in isolation to ensure they behave as expected.

1. Best Practices for Writing Unit Tests

- **Isolate Tests**: Each test should focus on a single unit of code. Avoid dependencies on other parts of the application.
- **Use Descriptive Names**: Name your tests clearly to describe what they are testing.
- **Mock Dependencies**: Use mocks or stubs for external dependencies to isolate the unit being tested.
- **Keep Tests Fast**: Ensure that your tests run quickly to provide immediate feedback.

2. Writing Unit Tests for Components

When testing components, focus on verifying their behavior and rendering logic.

Example of a Simple Component:

Let's create a basic CounterComponent that increments a counter when a button is clicked.

```typescript
Copy code
import { Component } from '@angular/core';

@Component({
  selector: 'app-counter',
  template: `
    <button (click)="increment()">Increment</button>
    <p>Counter: {{ counter }}</p>
  `
})
export class CounterComponent {
  counter = 0;

  increment() {
    this.counter++;
  }
}
```

Now, let's write unit tests for this component:

```typescript
Copy code
import { ComponentFixture, TestBed } from '@angular/core/testing';
import { CounterComponent } from './counter.component';

describe('CounterComponent', () => {
  let component: CounterComponent;
  let fixture: ComponentFixture<CounterComponent>;

  beforeEach(() => {
    TestBed.configureTestingModule({
      declarations: [CounterComponent]
    });

    fixture = TestBed.createComponent(CounterComponent);
    component = fixture.componentInstance;
  });

  it('should increment counter on button click', () => {
    component.increment();
    expect(component.counter).toBe(1);
  });

  it('should display the current counter value', () => {
    component.increment();
    fixture.detectChanges(); // Update the view
    const compiled = fixture.nativeElement;
    expect(compiled.querySelector('p').textContent).toContain('Counter: 1');
  });
});
```

In these tests:

- We verify that the increment() method correctly updates the counter.
- We check that the component displays the correct counter value in the template.

3. Writing Unit Tests for Services

Services are typically easier to test because they are isolated from the UI.

Example of a Simple Service:

Let's create a MathService that provides a method to add two numbers.

```typescript
Copy code
import { Injectable } from '@angular/core';

@Injectable({
  providedIn: 'root'
})
export class MathService {
  add(a: number, b: number): number {
    return a + b;
  }
}
```

Now, let's write unit tests for this service:

```typescript
Copy code
import { TestBed } from '@angular/core/testing';
import { MathService } from './math.service';

describe('MathService', () => {
  let service: MathService;

  beforeEach(() => {
    TestBed.configureTestingModule({});
    service = TestBed.inject(MathService);
  });

  it('should add two numbers correctly', () => {
    expect(service.add(2, 3)).toEqual(5);
    expect(service.add(-1, 1)).toEqual(0);
  });
});
```

In this test, we verify that the add method returns the correct result for various inputs.

Integration Testing in Angular

Integration testing focuses on testing the interactions between multiple components or services. The goal is to ensure that different parts of the application work together correctly.

1. Writing Integration Tests

When writing integration tests, you typically test the interactions between components and services.

Example of a Component Using a Service:

Let's create a ProductService that fetches products and a ProductListComponent that displays them.

```typescript
Copy code
import { Injectable } from '@angular/core';
import { Observable, of } from 'rxjs';

@Injectable({
  providedIn: 'root'
})
export class ProductService {
  getProducts(): Observable<Product[]> {
    return of([{ id: 1, name: 'Product A' }, { id: 2, name:
    'Product B' }]);
  }
}
```

Now, let's create a ProductListComponent:

```typescript
Copy code
import { Component, OnInit } from '@angular/core';
import { ProductService } from './product.service';
```

CHAPTER 11: MASTERING ANGULAR TESTING TECHNIQUES

```
@Component({
  selector: 'app-product-list',
  template: `
    <ul>
      <li *ngFor="let product of products">{{ product.name }}</li>
    </ul>
  `
})
export class ProductListComponent implements OnInit {
  products: Product[] = [];

  constructor(private productService: ProductService) {}

  ngOnInit() {
    this.productService.getProducts().subscribe(data => {
      this.products = data;
    });
  }
}
```

Now, let's write an integration test for this component:

```
typescript
Copy code
import { ComponentFixture, TestBed } from '@angular/core/testing';
import { ProductListComponent } from './product-list.component';
import { ProductService } from './product.service';
import { of } from 'rxjs';

class MockProductService {
  getProducts() {
    return of([{ id: 1, name: 'Product A' }, { id: 2, name:
    'Product B' }]);
  }
}

describe('ProductListComponent', () => {
  let component: ProductListComponent;
```

```
  let fixture: ComponentFixture<ProductListComponent>;

  beforeEach(() => {
    TestBed.configureTestingModule({
      declarations: [ProductListComponent],
      providers: [{ provide: ProductService, useClass:
      MockProductService }]
    });

    fixture = TestBed.createComponent(ProductListComponent);
    component = fixture.componentInstance;
  });

  it('should display a list of products', () => {
    fixture.detectChanges(); // Trigger data binding
    const compiled = fixture.nativeElement;
    expect(compiled.querySelectorAll('li').length).toBe(2);
    expect(compiled.querySelector('li').textContent).toContain('Product
    A');
  });
});
```

In this integration test:

- We use a mock version of ProductService to simulate the data retrieval.
- We verify that ProductListComponent correctly displays the products retrieved from the service.

End-to-End (E2E) Testing with Protractor

End-to-end testing simulates user interactions with your application to verify that everything works as expected from the user's perspective. Protractor is the primary framework used for E2E testing in Angular applications.

1. Writing E2E Tests

E2E tests are written in a way that simulates real user interactions. Here's how you can create a simple E2E test for the login functionality of your application.

CHAPTER 11: MASTERING ANGULAR TESTING TECHNIQUES

Example of a Simple Login E2E Test:

1. Set up a basic login page in your application.
2. Create a Protractor test in the e2e folder:

```typescript
Copy code
import { browser, by, element } from 'protractor';

describe('Login E2E Tests', () => {
  beforeEach(() => {
    browser.get('/login'); // Navigate to the login page
  });

  it('should log in with valid credentials', async () => {
    await element(by.id('username')).sendKeys('testuser');
    await element(by.id('password')).sendKeys('password123');
    await element(by.buttonText('Login')).click();

    const successMessage = await
    element(by.css('.success')).getText();
    expect(successMessage).toContain('Login successful');
  });

  it('should show an error message with invalid credentials',
  async () => {
    await element(by.id('username')).sendKeys('invaliduser');
    await element(by.id('password')).sendKeys('wrongpassword');
    await element(by.buttonText('Login')).click();

    const errorMessage = await element(by.css('.error')).getText();
    expect(errorMessage).toContain('Invalid credentials');
  });
});
```

In this E2E test:

- We navigate to the login page and simulate user input.

- We verify that the application displays the appropriate success or error messages based on the login attempt.

2. Running E2E Tests

To run your E2E tests, use the following command:

```bash
Copy code
ng e2e
```

This command will start the Protractor test runner, which executes your tests against the application.

Advanced Testing Techniques

As you become more experienced with testing in Angular, you can explore advanced techniques that enhance your testing strategy.

1. Testing Asynchronous Code

When testing components or services that involve asynchronous operations (e.g., HTTP requests), you can use the fakeAsync and tick utilities provided by Angular's testing library.

Example of Testing Asynchronous Code:

```typescript
Copy code
import { ComponentFixture, TestBed, fakeAsync, tick } from '@angular/core/testing';
import { ProductService } from './product.service';
import { ProductListComponent } from './product-list.component';
import { of } from 'rxjs';

class MockProductService {
  getProducts() {
    return of([{ id: 1, name: 'Product A' }]);
```

CHAPTER 11: MASTERING ANGULAR TESTING TECHNIQUES

```
  }
}

describe('ProductListComponent', () => {
  let component: ProductListComponent;
  let fixture: ComponentFixture<ProductListComponent>;

  beforeEach(() => {
    TestBed.configureTestingModule({
      declarations: [ProductListComponent],
      providers: [{ provide: ProductService, useClass:
      MockProductService }]
    });

    fixture = TestBed.createComponent(ProductListComponent);
    component = fixture.componentInstance;
  });

  it('should display products after async call', fakeAsync(() => {
    component.ngOnInit(); // Trigger ngOnInit
    tick(); // Simulate the passage of time for async operations
    fixture.detectChanges(); // Update the view

    const compiled = fixture.nativeElement;
    expect(compiled.querySelector('li').textContent).toContain('Product
    A');
  }));
});
```

In this test, we use fakeAsync to handle asynchronous calls, allowing us to simulate the passing of time with tick().

2. Using Spy Objects

Jasmine's spying capabilities allow you to track calls to functions and methods. This can be particularly useful for verifying interactions with services.

Example of Using Spies:

```typescript
Copy code
import { TestBed } from '@angular/core/testing';
import { ProductService } from './product.service';

describe('ProductService', () => {
  let service: ProductService;
  let httpClientSpy: { get: jasmine.Spy };

  beforeEach(() => {
    httpClientSpy = jasmine.createSpyObj('HttpClient', ['get']);
    service = new ProductService(httpClientSpy as any);
  });

  it('should call getProducts once', () => {
    service.getProducts();
    expect(httpClientSpy.get.calls.count()).toBe(1); // Verify the method was called once
  });
});
```

In this example, we use a spy object to track calls to the get method of HttpClient. This allows us to assert that the method is called when getProducts is invoked.

3. Testing Observables

When testing components and services that rely on Observables, ensure that you subscribe to them in your tests. This allows you to verify that the expected data flows through your application correctly.

Example of Testing Observables:

```typescript
Copy code
import { ComponentFixture, TestBed, fakeAsync, tick } from '@angular/core/testing';
import { ProductListComponent } from './product-list.component';
import { ProductService } from '../product.service';
import { of } from 'rxjs';
```

CHAPTER 11: MASTERING ANGULAR TESTING TECHNIQUES

```
class MockProductService {
  getProducts() {
    return of([{ id: 1, name: 'Product A' }]);
  }
}

describe('ProductListComponent', () => {
  let component: ProductListComponent;
  let fixture: ComponentFixture<ProductListComponent>;

  beforeEach(() => {
    TestBed.configureTestingModule({
      declarations: [ProductListComponent],
      providers: [{ provide: ProductService, useClass:
      MockProductService }]
    });

    fixture = TestBed.createComponent(ProductListComponent);
    component = fixture.componentInstance;
  });

  it('should display products after async call', fakeAsync(() => {
    component.ngOnInit(); // Trigger ngOnInit
    tick(); // Simulate the passage of time for async operations
    fixture.detectChanges(); // Update the view

    const compiled = fixture.nativeElement;
    expect(compiled.querySelector('li').textContent).toContain('Product
    A');
  }));
});
```

In this test, we ensure that the component correctly handles the observable returned by the service.

Performance Testing

In addition to functional testing, performance testing is essential to ensure that your Angular application meets performance requirements. You can use various tools and techniques to monitor and measure performance.

1. Angular Performance Tools

Angular provides several built-in tools for monitoring and improving performance:

- **Angular DevTools**: A browser extension that allows you to inspect the structure of Angular applications and analyze change detection cycles.
- **Profiler**: Use the built-in performance profiling tools in modern browsers (e.g., Chrome DevTools) to analyze the performance of your application and identify rendering issues.

2. Measuring Performance Metrics

Use tools like Google Lighthouse to measure performance metrics such as First Contentful Paint (FCP), Time to Interactive (TTI), and Speed Index. Lighthouse can be run directly in Chrome DevTools or as a command-line tool.

Running Lighthouse in Chrome DevTools:

1. Open Chrome DevTools (F12).
2. Go to the "Lighthouse" tab.
3. Select the metrics you want to measure and click "Generate report."

Lighthouse provides a comprehensive report on performance, accessibility, and SEO, helping you identify areas for improvement.

Conclusion

In this chapter, we covered various Angular testing techniques, including unit testing, integration testing, and end-to-end testing. We explored best practices for writing tests, how to set up your testing environment, and advanced testing strategies.

Testing is an essential part of Angular development that helps ensure the quality and reliability of your applications. By mastering testing techniques, you can improve the maintainability of your code, boost developer confidence, and enhance user satisfaction.

Chapter 12: Deploying Angular Applications

Deploying an Angular application is the process of making it available for users. This involves several steps, from building the application for production to choosing the right hosting environment, configuring the server, and managing updates. This chapter will provide a comprehensive guide on deploying Angular applications, focusing on best practices, tools, and strategies for a successful deployment.

Understanding the Deployment Process

The deployment process typically consists of several key steps:

1. **Building the Application**: Compiling the Angular application into optimized static files that can be served by a web server.
2. **Choosing a Hosting Environment**: Selecting the right platform to host your application (e.g., static hosting, cloud services).
3. **Configuring the Server**: Setting up the server to handle routing, SSL, and other configurations.
4. **Deploying the Application**: Uploading the built application files to the hosting environment.
5. **Managing Updates**: Implementing a strategy for rolling out updates and maintaining the application post-deployment.

CHAPTER 12: DEPLOYING ANGULAR APPLICATIONS

Understanding these steps is crucial for ensuring a smooth deployment.

Building the Angular Application for Production

Before deploying your Angular application, you need to build it for production. This process involves compiling and optimizing the application to ensure fast load times and a good user experience.

1. Building the Application

Angular CLI provides a straightforward command to build your application for production. The command compiles the application, bundles the files, and optimizes the output.

To build the application, run the following command:

```bash
Copy code
ng build --prod
```

Breakdown of the Build Command:

- **—prod**: This flag enables production optimizations, including:
- **Ahead-of-Time (AOT) Compilation**: Pre-compiles the application, reducing the size of the JavaScript bundles and improving load times.
- **Tree Shaking**: Removes unused code from the final bundle, decreasing the overall size of the application.
- **Minification**: Reduces file sizes by removing whitespace, comments, and renaming variables.

Example of Build Output:

After running the build command, Angular will generate a dist/ directory containing the compiled application. The structure will typically look like this:

```
css
Copy code
dist/
    your-app-name/
        index.html
        main.js
        polyfills.js
        runtime.js
        styles.css
        assets/
```

- **index.html**: The main entry point for your application.
- **main.js**: The main bundle containing your application logic.
- **styles.css**: Global styles for your application.
- **assets/**: Directory for images and other static files.

2. Managing Environment Configurations

Angular allows you to manage different configurations for various environments (development, production, testing, etc.). You can define environment-specific variables in the src/environments directory.

Example of Environment Files:

1. **src/environments/environment.ts** (Development):

```
typescript
Copy code
export const environment = {
  production: false,
  apiUrl: 'http://localhost:3000/api'
};
```

1. **src/environments/environment.prod.ts** (Production):

```typescript
Copy code
export const environment = {
  production: true,
  apiUrl: 'https://api.yourapp.com'
};
```

During the build process, Angular replaces the environment file based on the configuration, ensuring that the correct settings are used in production.

Choosing a Hosting Environment

The next step in the deployment process is selecting a suitable hosting environment for your Angular application. There are various options available, each with its advantages and use cases.

1. Static Hosting Services

Static hosting services are ideal for serving Angular applications since they primarily consist of static files (HTML, CSS, JS). Popular static hosting services include:

- **GitHub Pages**: A free hosting service that allows you to publish your application directly from a GitHub repository.
- **Netlify**: A platform for hosting static sites with features like continuous deployment, custom domains, and form handling.
- **Vercel**: Another static hosting service that supports automatic deployments from Git repositories and offers serverless functions.
- **Firebase Hosting**: A part of Google's Firebase platform that provides fast and secure hosting for static content.

Example of Deploying to Netlify:

To deploy your Angular application to Netlify:

1. Create a new site on the Netlify dashboard.

2. Link your GitHub repository or drag and drop your dist/ folder onto the Netlify dashboard.
3. Configure the build settings to use ng build —prod as the build command and set the publish directory to dist/your-app-name.

2. Cloud Services

Cloud services provide more flexibility and scalability for hosting Angular applications. These platforms allow you to host dynamic applications and offer additional features like databases, server-side processing, and custom domain support. Some popular cloud services include:

- **Amazon Web Services (AWS)**: A comprehensive cloud computing platform offering services like Amazon S3 for static hosting and AWS Amplify for full-stack applications.
- **Microsoft Azure**: A cloud platform that provides Azure App Service for hosting web applications, including Angular applications.
- **Google Cloud Platform (GCP)**: Offers Google App Engine and Cloud Storage for hosting applications and static assets.

Example of Deploying to AWS S3:

To deploy your Angular application to AWS S3:

1. Build your application using ng build —prod.
2. Create an S3 bucket in the AWS Management Console.
3. Upload the contents of the dist/your-app-name directory to the S3 bucket.
4. Configure the bucket for static website hosting by enabling public access and setting the index document (usually index.html).

3. Traditional Web Hosting

You can also deploy Angular applications on traditional web hosting services, such as shared hosting or virtual private servers (VPS). In this case, you typically need to configure your web server (e.g., Apache, Nginx) to serve the Angular application correctly.

Example of Deploying to Apache:

1. Build your Angular application using ng build —prod.
2. Upload the contents of the dist/your-app-name directory to your web server's root directory.
3. Create an .htaccess file in the root directory to handle routing:

```apache
Copy code
<IfModule mod_rewrite.c>
  RewriteEngine On
  RewriteBase /
  RewriteRule ^index\.html$ - [L]
  RewriteCond %{REQUEST_FILENAME} !-f
  RewriteCond %{REQUEST_FILENAME} !-d
  RewriteRule . /index.html [L]
</IfModule>
```

This configuration ensures that all routes are redirected to index.html, allowing Angular's router to handle navigation.

Configuring the Server

After choosing a hosting environment, the next step is configuring the server to serve your Angular application correctly.

1. Configuring Routing for Single-Page Applications

Angular applications are single-page applications (SPAs), meaning they use client-side routing. When users refresh a page or navigate directly to a URL, the server must be configured to serve the index.html file for all routes.

Example of Nginx Configuration:

If you are using Nginx as your web server, you can configure it as follows:

```nginx
Copy code
server {
    listen 80;
    server_name yourdomain.com;

    location / {
        root /path/to/your/dist/your-app-name;
        try_files $uri $uri/ /index.html;  # Serve index.html for
        all routes
    }

    error_page 404 /index.html;  # Handle 404 errors by serving
    index.html
}
```

This configuration ensures that all requests are routed through index.html, allowing Angular's router to handle navigation.

2. Environment Variables

When deploying applications to cloud services, you may need to manage environment variables to store sensitive information such as API keys and database connection strings.

- **AWS**: Use AWS Systems Manager Parameter Store or AWS Secrets Manager to manage sensitive information securely.
- **Azure**: Use Azure App Service settings to configure application settings and connection strings securely.
- **Firebase**: Firebase provides configuration options in the Firebase console to manage environment variables.

Deploying the Application

With the application built and the hosting environment configured, it's time to deploy your Angular application.

1. Manual Deployment

For simple projects or when using static hosting, you can deploy your

CHAPTER 12: DEPLOYING ANGULAR APPLICATIONS

application manually by uploading the contents of the dist/ directory to your hosting service using an FTP client, web interface, or command-line tool.

2. Continuous Deployment

For larger projects or team environments, implementing continuous deployment (CD) is beneficial. Continuous deployment automates the process of deploying your application whenever changes are pushed to your repository.

Example of Setting Up Continuous Deployment with GitHub Actions:

1. Create a .github/workflows/deploy.yml file in your repository:

```yaml
Copy code
name: Deploy Angular App

on:
  push:
    branches:
      - main   # Deploy on push to the main branch

jobs:
  build-and-deploy:
    runs-on: ubuntu-latest

    steps:
      - name: Checkout code
        uses: actions/checkout@v2

      - name: Set up Node.js
        uses: actions/setup-node@v2
        with:
          node-version: '14'   # Specify the Node.js version

      - name: Install dependencies
        run: npm install

      - name: Build the app
```

```
      run: npm run build --prod

    - name: Deploy to Netlify
      uses: nwtgck/actions-netlify@v1
      with:
        publish-dir: ./dist/your-app-name
        production-deploy: true
        github-token: ${{ secrets.GITHUB_TOKEN }}
        netlify-token: ${{ secrets.NETLIFY_TOKEN }}  # Add your
        Netlify token as a secret
```

1. Add the NETLIFY_TOKEN as a secret in your GitHub repository settings.

This GitHub Action will automatically build and deploy your Angular application to Netlify whenever changes are pushed to the main branch.

Monitoring and Maintaining the Application

After deploying your application, it's essential to monitor its performance and make regular updates to ensure it runs smoothly.

1. Monitoring Application Performance

Monitoring tools help you keep track of your application's performance and identify issues in real-time. Some popular monitoring tools include:

- **Google Analytics**: Provides insights into user behavior and application usage.
- **Sentry**: A monitoring tool that tracks errors and performance issues in real-time.
- **New Relic**: Offers application performance monitoring and analytics to optimize performance.

2. Handling Updates

As your application evolves, you'll need to deploy updates regularly. Follow

CHAPTER 12: DEPLOYING ANGULAR APPLICATIONS

these steps to manage updates effectively:

- **Version Control**: Use version control systems like Git to track changes and manage code versions.
- **Build and Deploy**: Follow the same build and deployment processes for updates as you did for the initial deployment.
- **Rollback Strategy**: Have a rollback strategy in place in case a deployment introduces critical bugs. This could involve keeping previous builds available for redeployment.

3. User Feedback and Continuous Improvement

Encourage users to provide feedback on their experience with your application. User feedback is invaluable for identifying areas for improvement and enhancing user satisfaction.

- **Surveys and Forms**: Implement surveys and feedback forms to gather user insights.
- **User Interviews**: Conduct user interviews to gain deeper insights into user needs and pain points.

Best Practices for Angular Deployment

To ensure a smooth deployment process and optimal application performance, consider the following best practices:

1. **Automate Deployment**: Use CI/CD pipelines to automate the deployment process, reducing manual errors and saving time.
2. **Optimize Assets**: Compress and optimize assets such as images and stylesheets to reduce loading times.
3. **Use a CDN**: Consider using a Content Delivery Network (CDN) to distribute static assets globally, reducing latency and improving load times.
4. **Implement Security Measures**: Ensure that your application follows best security practices, including HTTPS, secure headers, and regular security

updates.

5. **Test Before Deploying**: Always run tests (unit, integration, and E2E) before deploying to catch potential issues early.
6. **Monitor Performance**: Continuously monitor your application's performance and user feedback to identify areas for improvement.
7. **Maintain Documentation**: Keep your deployment processes and configurations well-documented for easier onboarding of new team members.

Conclusion

In this chapter, we covered the essential aspects of deploying Angular applications, including building for production, choosing a hosting environment, configuring the server, and managing updates. By following the strategies and best practices outlined in this chapter, you can ensure a successful deployment process and maintain optimal performance for your Angular applications.

Chapter 13: Advanced Angular Development Techniques

As you advance in your Angular development journey, it's essential to explore techniques that enhance your applications' performance, maintainability, and scalability. This chapter will cover advanced concepts, including best practices for building scalable applications, creating reusable components, leveraging Angular features for performance optimization, and implementing state management with NgRx. By mastering these techniques, you will be better equipped to tackle complex Angular projects.

Building Scalable Applications

Scalability is a crucial aspect of application development. As your application grows, you need to ensure it can handle increased traffic, data, and user interactions without compromising performance. Here are several strategies to build scalable Angular applications.

1. Modular Architecture

Adopting a modular architecture is one of the most effective ways to ensure scalability. This involves organizing your application into cohesive, independent modules that encapsulate specific functionality.

- **Core Module**: Contains singleton services that are used throughout the application. For example, authentication services, logging services, etc.
- **Shared Module**: Contains common components, directives, and pipes that can be reused across multiple feature modules. This helps avoid code duplication and promotes consistency.
- **Feature Modules**: Each feature of your application should have its own module. For instance, you might have UserModule, ProductModule, and OrderModule, each containing components and services related to that feature.

Example of a Feature Module:

Generate a new feature module using the Angular CLI:

```bash
Copy code
ng generate module user --routing
```

In the user.module.ts, declare components and import necessary modules:

```typescript
Copy code
import { NgModule } from '@angular/core';
import { CommonModule } from '@angular/common';
import { UserRoutingModule } from './user-routing.module';
import { UserComponent } from './user.component';

@NgModule({
  declarations: [UserComponent],
  imports: [
    CommonModule,
    UserRoutingModule
  ]
})
export class UserModule {}
```

By organizing your application this way, you enhance maintainability and make it easier to scale as new features are added.

2. Lazy Loading Modules

Lazy loading is an optimization technique that defers the loading of feature modules until they are needed. This helps reduce the initial load time of your application.

Setting Up Lazy Loading:

To implement lazy loading, define routes for lazy-loaded modules in your routing module:

```typescript
Copy code
const routes: Routes = [
  { path: 'users', loadChildren: () =>
  import('./user/user.module').then(m => m.UserModule) },
  { path: 'products', loadChildren: () =>
  import('./product/product.module').then(m => m.ProductModule) },
];
```

When a user navigates to /users, the UserModule is loaded asynchronously, improving the initial load performance of your application.

3. Service-Oriented Architecture

Embrace a service-oriented architecture by encapsulating business logic and data access in services. This separation of concerns makes it easier to test, maintain, and reuse code.

Example of a Service:

Create a UserService that manages user-related operations:

```typescript
Copy code
import { Injectable } from '@angular/core';
import { HttpClient } from '@angular/common/http';
import { Observable } from 'rxjs';

@Injectable({
  providedIn: 'root'
})
```

```
export class UserService {
  private apiUrl = 'https://api.example.com/users';

  constructor(private http: HttpClient) {}

  getUsers(): Observable<User[]> {
    return this.http.get<User[]>(this.apiUrl);
  }

  getUserById(id: number): Observable<User> {
    return this.http.get<User>(`${this.apiUrl}/${id}`);
  }
}
```

By centralizing data management in services, you can maintain a clean and organized codebase, making it easier to scale as your application grows.

Creating Reusable Components

Reusable components are vital for maintaining a consistent user interface and reducing code duplication. By designing components that can be easily reused across your application, you can enhance development efficiency and simplify maintenance.

1. Designing Reusable Components

When creating reusable components, keep the following principles in mind:

- **Encapsulate Logic and Styles**: Ensure that your components encapsulate their logic and styles to avoid conflicts with other parts of the application.
- **Use Input and Output Properties**: Utilize @Input() and @Output() decorators to allow parent components to pass data to child components and emit events back to parent components.
- **Provide Default Values**: Set default values for @Input() properties to enhance usability and provide sensible defaults for consumers of the component.

Example of a Reusable Modal Component:

Here's an example of a reusable modal component:

```typescript
Copy code
import { Component, Input, Output, EventEmitter } from '@angular/core';

@Component({
  selector: 'app-modal',
  template: `
    <div class="modal">
      <div class="modal-content">
        <span class="close" (click)="close()">&times;</span>
        <h2>{{ title }}</h2>
        <ng-content></ng-content>
        <button (click)="confirm()">Confirm</button>
      </div>
    </div>
  `,
  styles: [`
    .modal { display: block; /* Full-screen modal styles */ }
    .modal-content { /* Modal content styles */ }
    .close { cursor: pointer; }
  `]
})
export class ModalComponent {
  @Input() title: string = 'Modal Title';
  @Output() onClose = new EventEmitter<void>();
  @Output() onConfirm = new EventEmitter<void>();

  close() {
    this.onClose.emit();
  }

  confirm() {
    this.onConfirm.emit();
  }
}
```

In this example:

- The modal component encapsulates its styles and logic.
- It uses @Input() for the title and @Output() to emit events for closing and confirming the modal.

2. Using Angular Material for Reusable UI Components

Angular Material provides a comprehensive set of pre-built UI components that adhere to Material Design principles. Using Angular Material can significantly speed up development and improve the consistency of your application's UI.

Example of Using Angular Material Dialog:

To create a reusable dialog component using Angular Material:

1. Install Angular Material if you haven't done so already:

```bash
Copy code
ng add @angular/material
```

1. Import the Material dialog module in your app module:

```typescript
Copy code
import { MatDialogModule } from '@angular/material/dialog';

@NgModule({
  imports: [MatDialogModule],
})
export class AppModule {}
```

CHAPTER 13: ADVANCED ANGULAR DEVELOPMENT TECHNIQUES

1. Create a dialog component:

```typescript
Copy code
import { Component } from '@angular/core';
import { MatDialogRef } from '@angular/material/dialog';

@Component({
  selector: 'app-dialog',
  template: `
    <h1 mat-dialog-title>Dialog Title</h1>
    <div mat-dialog-content>
      <p>Dialog content goes here.</p>
    </div>
    <div mat-dialog-actions>
      <button mat-button (click)="onClose()">Close</button>
    </div>
})
export class DialogComponent {
  constructor(public dialogRef: MatDialogRef<DialogComponent>) {}

  onClose(): void {
    this.dialogRef.close();
  }
}
```

1. Open the dialog from another component:

```typescript
Copy code
import { Component } from '@angular/core';
import { MatDialog } from '@angular/material/dialog';
import { DialogComponent } from './dialog.component';
```

```
@Component({
  selector: 'app-example',
  template: `<button (click)="openDialog()">Open Dialog</button>`
})
export class ExampleComponent {
  constructor(public dialog: MatDialog) {}

  openDialog(): void {
    this.dialog.open(DialogComponent);
  }
}
```

Using Angular Material components helps you maintain a consistent UI while also speeding up development.

Leveraging Angular Features for Performance Optimization

Angular offers several features that can help optimize application performance. Understanding and leveraging these features is essential for building high-performance applications.

1. Change Detection Strategy

Angular uses a change detection mechanism to update the UI based on data changes. Understanding and optimizing this process can significantly improve performance.

- **Default Change Detection**: By default, Angular checks all components for changes, which can lead to performance issues in large applications.
- **OnPush Change Detection**: Use ChangeDetectionStrategy.OnPush to optimize components that do not change often. With this strategy, Angular checks the component only when its input properties change or an event occurs.

Example of Using OnPush:

```typescript
Copy code
import { Component, ChangeDetectionStrategy } from '@angular/core';

@Component({
  selector: 'app-optimized',
  template: `<div>{{ data }}</div>`,
  changeDetection: ChangeDetectionStrategy.OnPush
})
export class OptimizedComponent {
  data = 'Optimized Data';
}
```

By adopting the OnPush strategy, you can reduce the number of checks Angular performs, improving performance.

2. TrackBy Function in ngFor

When rendering lists with *ngFor, Angular must check every item in the array for changes. Using a trackBy function can help optimize this process.

Example of Using trackBy:

```html
Copy code
<ul>
  <li *ngFor="let item of items; trackBy: trackById">{{ item.name }}</li>
</ul>
```
```typescript
Copy code
trackById(index: number, item: Item): number {
  return item.id; // Return unique identifier for the item
}
```

Using trackBy helps Angular track changes more efficiently and improves rendering performance.

3. Lazy Loading Modules

Lazy loading is an optimization technique that defers the loading of feature modules until they are needed. This helps reduce the initial load time of your application.

Setting Up Lazy Loading:

To implement lazy loading, define routes for lazy-loaded modules in your routing module:

```typescript
Copy code
const routes: Routes = [
  { path: 'feature', loadChildren: () =>
  import('./feature/feature.module').then(m => m.FeatureModule) },
];
```

When a user navigates to the /feature route, the FeatureModule is loaded asynchronously, improving the initial load performance of your application.

4. Using Web Workers

Web Workers allow you to run scripts in background threads, freeing up the main thread for UI interactions. This is useful for performing computationally intensive tasks without blocking the user interface.

Example of Using Web Workers:

1. Generate a Web Worker using Angular CLI:

```bash
Copy code
ng generate web-worker my-worker
```

1. In your worker file (my-worker.worker.ts), you can perform background tasks:

CHAPTER 13: ADVANCED ANGULAR DEVELOPMENT TECHNIQUES

```typescript
Copy code
addEventListener('message', ({ data }) => {
  const result = performHeavyComputation(data);
  postMessage(result);
});

function performHeavyComputation(input: number): number {
  // Simulate heavy computation
  return input * 1000;
}
```

1. In your component, you can use the worker:

```typescript
Copy code
const worker = new Worker(new URL('./my-worker.worker',
import.meta.url));
worker.onmessage = ({ data }) => {
  console.log('Result from worker:', data);
};
worker.postMessage(42);
```

Using Web Workers helps keep your application responsive while performing heavy computations in the background.

Implementing State Management with NgRx

As applications grow in complexity, managing state becomes increasingly challenging. NgRx provides a powerful state management solution for Angular applications based on the Redux pattern.

1. **Overview of NgRx**

NgRx provides a set of tools for managing application state, including actions, reducers, selectors, and effects. This structured approach helps maintain predictable state management across the application.

Key Concepts of NgRx:

- **Store**: The central repository that holds the application state. It acts as a single source of truth for the entire application.
- **Actions**: Objects that represent events in the application. Actions are dispatched to the store to indicate that something has happened.
- **Reducers**: Pure functions that specify how the application state changes in response to actions.
- **Selectors**: Functions that allow you to select specific slices of state from the store.
- **Effects**: Side effects are operations that interact with the outside world, such as making HTTP requests.

2. Setting Up NgRx

To get started with NgRx, you need to install the necessary packages and set up the store in your Angular application.

Installing NgRx Packages:

Run the following command to install NgRx:

```bash
Copy code
ng add @ngrx/store @ngrx/effects @ngrx/store-devtools
```

This command will install the core NgRx packages and set up the Store DevTools for debugging.

Configuring the Store:

In app.module.ts, import the necessary modules:

```typescript
Copy code
import { NgModule } from '@angular/core';
import { BrowserModule } from '@angular/platform-browser';
```

```
import { StoreModule } from '@ngrx/store';
import { EffectsModule } from '@ngrx/effects';
import { StoreDevtoolsModule } from '@ngrx/store-devtools';
import { AppComponent } from './app.component';
import { reducers } from './reducers'; // Import your reducers

@NgModule({
  declarations: [AppComponent],
  imports: [
    BrowserModule,
    StoreModule.forRoot(reducers),
    EffectsModule.forRoot([]),
    StoreDevtoolsModule.instrument({
      maxAge: 25,
      logOnly: environment.production,
    }),
  ],
  providers: [],
  bootstrap: [AppComponent],
})
export class AppModule {}
```

3. Creating Actions and Reducers

Actions represent events in your application, while reducers specify how the state changes in response to those actions.

Example of Creating Actions:

Create a file named user.actions.ts:

```
typescript
Copy code
import { createAction, props } from '@ngrx/store';

export const loadUsers = createAction('[User API] Load Users');
export const loadUsersSuccess = createAction(
  '[User API] Load Users Success',
  props<{ users: User[] }>()
);
export const loadUsersFailure = createAction(
```

```
  '[User API] Load Users Failure',
  props<{ error: string }>()
);
```

Example of Creating Reducers:

Create a file named user.reducer.ts:

```typescript
Copy code
import { createReducer, on } from '@ngrx/store';
import { loadUsersSuccess, loadUsersFailure } from
'./user.actions';

export interface UserState {
  users: User[];
  error: string | null;
}

export const initialState: UserState = {
  users: [],
  error: null,
};

export const userReducer = createReducer(
  initialState,
  on(loadUsersSuccess, (state, { users }) => ({ ...state, users,
error: null })),
  on(loadUsersFailure, (state, { error }) => ({ ...state, error }))
);
```

4. Creating Selectors

Selectors allow you to retrieve specific pieces of state from the store.

Example of Creating Selectors:

Create a file named user.selectors.ts:

```typescript
Copy code
import { createFeatureSelector, createSelector } from 
'@ngrx/store';
import { UserState } from './user.reducer';

export const selectUserState = 
createFeatureSelector<UserState>('user');

export const selectAllUsers = createSelector(
  selectUserState,
  (state: UserState) => state.users
);

export const selectUserError = createSelector(
  selectUserState,
  (state: UserState) => state.error
);
```

5. Using NgRx Effects

NgRx Effects allow you to handle side effects, such as making API calls.

Example of Creating Effects:

Create a file named user.effects.ts:

```typescript
Copy code
import { Injectable } from '@angular/core';
import { Actions, createEffect, ofType } from '@ngrx/effects';
import { UserService } from './user.service';
import { loadUsers, loadUsersSuccess, loadUsersFailure } from 
'./user.actions';
import { catchError, map, mergeMap } from 'rxjs/operators';
import { of } from 'rxjs';

@Injectable()
export class UserEffects {
  constructor(
    private actions$: Actions,
```

```
    private userService: UserService
  ) {}

  loadUsers$ = createEffect(() =>
    this.actions$.pipe(
      ofType(loadUsers),
      mergeMap(() =>
        this.userService.getUsers().pipe(
          map(users => loadUsersSuccess({ users })),
          catchError(error => of(loadUsersFailure({ error })))
        )
      )
    )
  );
}
```

In this example:

- We listen for the loadUsers action and call the UserService to fetch users.
- On success, we dispatch the loadUsersSuccess action; on failure, we dispatch the loadUsersFailure action.

Testing in Angular

Testing is an integral part of the development process. It ensures your application behaves as expected and helps prevent regressions. Angular provides powerful testing utilities that make it easier to test components, services, and other parts of your application.

1. Setting Up the Testing Environment

When you create an Angular application using the CLI, it comes with a preconfigured testing environment that includes tools like Jasmine and Karma.

Example of Configuring Karma:

The configuration file for Karma is typically named karma.conf.js. You can customize it to specify which files to include, the testing framework, and the browsers to run the tests in.

Here's a basic example of a karma.conf.js file:

CHAPTER 13: ADVANCED ANGULAR DEVELOPMENT TECHNIQUES

```javascript
Copy code
module.exports = function(config) {
  config.set({
    basePath: '',
    frameworks: ['jasmine', '@angular-devkit/build-angular'],
    plugins: [
      require('karma-jasmine'),
      require('karma-chrome-launcher'),
      require('@angular-devkit/build-angular/plugins/karma')
    ],
    client: {
      clearContext: false // leave Jasmine Spec Runner output
      visible in browser
    },
    files: [
      // Add your test files and polyfills here
    ],
    preprocessors: {
      './src/**/*.spec.ts': ['coverage']
    },
    reporters: ['progress', 'coverage'],
    port: 9876,
    colors: true,
    logLevel: config.LOG_INFO,
    autoWatch: true,
    browsers: ['Chrome'],
    singleRun: false,
    restartOnFileChange: true
  });
};
```

2. Writing Unit Tests

Unit tests focus on testing individual components or services in isolation. The goal is to verify that each unit behaves as expected.

Example of Writing a Unit Test for a Component:

Let's write a unit test for the CounterComponent we defined earlier.

```typescript
import { ComponentFixture, TestBed } from '@angular/core/testing';
import { CounterComponent } from './counter.component';

describe('CounterComponent', () => {
  let component: CounterComponent;
  let fixture: ComponentFixture<CounterComponent>;

  beforeEach(() => {
    TestBed.configureTestingModule({
      declarations: [CounterComponent]
    });

    fixture = TestBed.createComponent(CounterComponent);
    component = fixture.componentInstance;
  });

  it('should increment the counter', () => {
    component.increment();
    expect(component.counter).toBe(1);
  });

  it('should display the counter value', () => {
    component.increment();
    fixture.detectChanges();
    const compiled = fixture.nativeElement;
    expect(compiled.querySelector('p').textContent).toContain('Counter: 1');
  });
});
```

In these tests:

- We verify that the increment() method correctly updates the counter.
- We check that the component displays the correct counter value in the template.

3. Writing Integration Tests

CHAPTER 13: ADVANCED ANGULAR DEVELOPMENT TECHNIQUES

Integration tests verify that different parts of your application work together correctly.

Example of Writing an Integration Test:

Let's test the ProductListComponent that uses the ProductService.

```typescript
Copy code
import { ComponentFixture, TestBed } from '@angular/core/testing';
import { ProductListComponent } from './product-list.component';
import { ProductService } from './product.service';
import { of } from 'rxjs';

class MockProductService {
  getProducts() {
    return of([{ id: 1, name: 'Product A' }]);
  }
}

describe('ProductListComponent', () => {
  let component: ProductListComponent;
  let fixture: ComponentFixture<ProductListComponent>;

  beforeEach(() => {
    TestBed.configureTestingModule({
      declarations: [ProductListComponent],
      providers: [{ provide: ProductService, useClass:
      MockProductService }]
    });

    fixture = TestBed.createComponent(ProductListComponent);
    component = fixture.componentInstance;
  });

  it('should display products from the service', () => {
    fixture.detectChanges(); // Trigger data binding
    const compiled = fixture.nativeElement;
    expect(compiled.querySelector('li').textContent).toContain('Product
    A');
  });
```

```
});
```

In this integration test:

- We use a mock version of ProductService to simulate the data retrieval.
- We verify that ProductListComponent correctly displays the products retrieved from the service.

Conclusion

In this chapter, we explored advanced Angular development techniques, including strategies for building scalable applications, creating reusable components, leveraging Angular features for performance optimization, and implementing state management with NgRx.

By mastering these techniques, you can enhance the performance, maintainability, and scalability of your Angular applications, positioning yourself as a proficient Angular developer ready to tackle complex projects.

Chapter 14: Security Best Practices for Angular Applications

As web applications become increasingly complex and integral to business operations, ensuring their security has become a paramount concern for developers. Angular, as a popular framework, provides various built-in features and tools to help safeguard your applications against common vulnerabilities. In this chapter, we will explore the essential security best practices for Angular applications, including authentication, authorization, protecting against common attacks, secure coding practices, and strategies for maintaining application security. By the end of this chapter, you will be equipped with the knowledge to build secure Angular applications that protect user data and maintain integrity.

Understanding Application Security

Application security involves the measures and practices employed to prevent unauthorized access, use, disclosure, disruption, modification, or destruction of information within an application. Given the increasing number of cyber threats, it is essential to incorporate security into the software development lifecycle from the outset.

1. Common Security Vulnerabilities

Understanding common security vulnerabilities is the first step toward mitigating risks. Here are some prevalent threats:

- **Cross-Site Scripting (XSS)**: Attackers inject malicious scripts into webpages viewed by users. This can lead to data theft or session hijacking.
- **Cross-Site Request Forgery (CSRF)**: This attack tricks the user into submitting a request to a different site where they are authenticated, leading to unwanted actions.
- **SQL Injection**: Attackers manipulate SQL queries to gain unauthorized access to the database, potentially exposing sensitive data.
- **Insecure Direct Object References**: When an application exposes references to internal implementation objects, attackers can modify these references to access unauthorized data.
- **Security Misconfiguration**: Poorly configured security settings can expose applications to various attacks.

2. **The Importance of Security in Angular Applications**

Angular applications, like all web applications, face various security threats. Protecting user data and application integrity is vital for maintaining user trust and compliance with regulations (e.g., GDPR). Implementing security best practices helps prevent data breaches, enhances the reputation of your application, and reduces the risk of financial losses due to security incidents.

Implementing Authentication and Authorization

Authentication and authorization are critical components of application security. Authentication verifies the identity of users, while authorization determines their access rights.

1. **Authentication in Angular**

Angular applications typically use token-based authentication, where the server issues a token (e.g., JWT) upon successful login. This token is then sent with each subsequent request to verify the user's identity.

Example of Setting Up Authentication:

CHAPTER 14: SECURITY BEST PRACTICES FOR ANGULAR APPLICATIONS

1. **User Login**: Create a login form that captures the user's credentials.

```typescript
Copy code
import { Component } from '@angular/core';
import { AuthService } from './auth.service';

@Component({
  selector: 'app-login',
  template: `
    <form (submit)="login()">
      <input type="text" [(ngModel)]="username"
      placeholder="Username" required />
      <input type="password" [(ngModel)]="password"
      placeholder="Password" required />
      <button type="submit">Login</button>
    </form>
  `,
})
export class LoginComponent {
  username: string;
  password: string;

  constructor(private authService: AuthService) {}

  login() {
    this.authService.login(this.username, this.password);
  }
}
```

1. **AuthService**: Create a service to handle authentication logic.

```typescript
Copy code
```

```typescript
import { Injectable } from '@angular/core';
import { HttpClient } from '@angular/common/http';
import { Router } from '@angular/router';

@Injectable({
  providedIn: 'root',
})
export class AuthService {
  private apiUrl = 'https://api.example.com/auth';

  constructor(private http: HttpClient, private router: Router) {}

  login(username: string, password: string) {
    this.http.post(`${this.apiUrl}/login`, { username, password
    }).subscribe(
      (response: any) => {
        localStorage.setItem('token', response.token);
        this.router.navigate(['/dashboard']);
      },
      (error) => {
        console.error('Login failed', error);
      }
    );
  }

  logout() {
    localStorage.removeItem('token');
    this.router.navigate(['/login']);
  }

  isAuthenticated(): boolean {
    return !!localStorage.getItem('token');
  }
}
```

In this example:

- The AuthService handles user authentication and stores the token in local storage upon successful login.

2. Authorization in Angular

Authorization ensures that users have the correct permissions to access specific resources. Implementing route guards is a common way to enforce authorization in Angular applications.

Example of Implementing Route Guards:

1. **Create an Auth Guard**:

```typescript
Copy code
import { Injectable } from '@angular/core';
import { CanActivate, Router } from '@angular/router';
import { AuthService } from './auth.service';

@Injectable({
  providedIn: 'root',
})
export class AuthGuard implements CanActivate {
  constructor(private authService: AuthService, private router: Router) {}

  canActivate(): boolean {
    if (this.authService.isAuthenticated()) {
      return true;
    }
    this.router.navigate(['/login']);
    return false;
  }
}
```

1. **Apply the Guard to Routes**:

```typescript
Copy code
const routes: Routes = [
  { path: 'dashboard', component: DashboardComponent, canActivate: [AuthGuard] },
  { path: 'login', component: LoginComponent },
];
```

This setup ensures that only authenticated users can access the dashboard route.

Protecting Against Common Attacks

Protecting your application against common web attacks is essential for maintaining security. Here are several strategies to safeguard against these vulnerabilities.

1. Protecting Against XSS Attacks

Cross-site scripting (XSS) occurs when an attacker injects malicious scripts into web pages. Angular provides built-in protections against XSS, but you must follow best practices to ensure your application remains secure.

- **Use Angular's Sanitization**: Angular automatically sanitizes untrusted values in templates. Always bind dynamic values using Angular's binding syntax ({{ }}) rather than directly manipulating the DOM.
- **Avoid innerHTML**: Refrain from using innerHTML for displaying user input. If necessary, sanitize it using Angular's DomSanitizer.

Example of Using DomSanitizer:

```typescript
Copy code
import { Component } from '@angular/core';
import { DomSanitizer } from '@angular/platform-browser';
```

```
@Component({
  selector: 'app-safe-html',
  template: `<div [innerHTML]="safeHtml"></div>`,
})
export class SafeHtmlComponent {
  safeHtml: any;

  constructor(private sanitizer: DomSanitizer) {
    const html = '<p>Safe HTML content</p>'; // User-generated
    content
    this.safeHtml = this.sanitizer.bypassSecurityTrustHtml(html);
  }
}
```

2. Protecting Against CSRF Attacks

Cross-Site Request Forgery (CSRF) tricks users into submitting unauthorized requests. To protect against CSRF, you can implement the following strategies:

- **Use CSRF Tokens**: Implement CSRF tokens in your backend and require them for state-changing requests (e.g., POST, PUT, DELETE).
- **SameSite Cookies**: Set the SameSite attribute on cookies to prevent them from being sent along with cross-site requests.

3. Secure Coding Practices

Adopting secure coding practices is vital for preventing security vulnerabilities. Here are some best practices:

- **Validate User Input**: Always validate and sanitize user input to prevent injections. Implement both client-side and server-side validation.
- **Use HTTPS**: Always serve your application over HTTPS to encrypt data in transit and protect against man-in-the-middle attacks.
- **Avoid Exposing Sensitive Data**: Do not expose sensitive data in client-side code. Use environment variables and secure storage mechanisms for sensitive information.

- **Limit User Permissions**: Implement the principle of least privilege by granting users only the permissions necessary for their roles.

Securing API Endpoints

When building applications that interact with backend APIs, securing those endpoints is essential. Here are some strategies to secure your APIs:

1. Implement Authentication and Authorization

Use token-based authentication (e.g., JWT) to secure API endpoints. Require tokens for accessing protected routes and validate them on the server.

2. Rate Limiting

Implement rate limiting on your APIs to prevent abuse and DDoS attacks. Rate limiting restricts the number of requests a user can make within a certain timeframe.

3. Input Validation

Validate all incoming requests on your API. Ensure that input data adheres to expected formats, types, and lengths to prevent injections and other attacks.

4. Use Security Headers

Configure your API to use security headers to mitigate attacks:

- **Content Security Policy (CSP)**: Helps prevent XSS by controlling which resources can be loaded.
- **X-Content-Type-Options**: Prevents browsers from interpreting files as a different MIME type.
- **X-Frame-Options**: Protects against clickjacking by preventing the page from being displayed in a frame.

Implementing Secure Authentication Practices

Ensuring secure authentication practices is essential for protecting user accounts and sensitive data.

1. Strong Password Policies

Encourage users to create strong passwords by implementing password policies, such as:

- Minimum password length (e.g., at least 8 characters).
- Use of uppercase, lowercase, numbers, and special characters.
- Regular password changes.

2. Multi-Factor Authentication (MFA)

Implement multi-factor authentication to add an extra layer of security. MFA requires users to verify their identity through multiple methods (e.g., SMS, email, authenticator apps) before granting access.

Chapter 15: Building and Maintaining High-Performance Angular Applications

As web applications become more complex, ensuring they perform well is crucial for user experience and satisfaction. Angular provides powerful tools and features to create responsive and high-performance applications. This chapter will explore strategies for building and maintaining high-performance Angular applications, including optimizing rendering performance, managing application state, improving load times, and utilizing caching techniques. By the end of this chapter, you will be equipped with the knowledge to enhance your Angular applications' performance effectively.

Understanding Application Performance

Performance is the measure of how quickly and efficiently an application responds to user actions and delivers results. In the context of Angular applications, performance encompasses several factors, including load times, rendering speed, responsiveness, and user experience.

1. Key Performance Metrics

To gauge the performance of your Angular applications, it's essential to understand and measure the following metrics:

- **First Contentful Paint (FCP)**: Measures the time taken for the first piece of content to appear on the screen. A faster FCP indicates a more responsive application.
- **Time to Interactive (TTI)**: Indicates how long it takes for the application to become fully interactive. A lower TTI means that users can start interacting with the application sooner.
- **Speed Index**: Measures how quickly the contents of a page are visibly populated. A lower speed index signifies a better user experience.
- **Total Blocking Time (TBT)**: Measures the total amount of time that a page is blocked from responding to user input. Minimizing TBT helps improve user interaction.
- **Cumulative Layout Shift (CLS)**: Measures visual stability and how often users experience unexpected layout shifts. A lower CLS value indicates a more stable UI.

2. The Importance of Performance Optimization

Optimizing application performance is essential for several reasons:

- **User Satisfaction**: Fast-loading applications enhance user experience, leading to higher satisfaction and engagement rates.
- **Search Engine Optimization (SEO)**: Performance is a factor in search engine ranking algorithms. Faster applications are more likely to rank higher in search results.
- **Conversion Rates**: Improved performance can lead to higher conversion rates, as users are more likely to complete actions (e.g., purchases) on fast-loading applications.
- **Reduced Resource Costs**: Optimized applications can reduce server and bandwidth costs, especially for large-scale applications.

Optimizing Rendering Performance

Rendering performance directly impacts how quickly the UI responds to changes and user interactions. Optimizing rendering performance involves minimizing the number of change detection cycles and efficiently updating the DOM.

1. Change Detection Strategy

Angular uses a change detection mechanism to update the UI based on data changes. Understanding how to optimize this process can significantly improve rendering performance.

- **Default Change Detection**: Angular checks all components for changes, which can lead to performance issues in large applications.
- **OnPush Change Detection**: Use ChangeDetectionStrategy.OnPush to optimize components that do not change often. With this strategy, Angular checks the component only when its input properties change or an event occurs.

Example of Using OnPush:

```typescript
Copy code
import { Component, ChangeDetectionStrategy } from '@angular/core';

@Component({
  selector: 'app-optimized',
  template: `<div>{{ data }}</div>`,
  changeDetection: ChangeDetectionStrategy.OnPush
})
export class OptimizedComponent {
  data = 'Optimized Data';
}
```

By adopting the OnPush strategy, you can reduce the number of checks Angular performs, improving performance.

2. Using TrackBy in ngFor

When rendering lists with *ngFor, Angular must check every item in the array for changes. Using a trackBy function can help optimize this process.

Example of Using trackBy:

```html
Copy code
<ul>
  <li *ngFor="let item of items; trackBy: trackById">{{ item.name }}</li>
</ul>
```

```typescript
Copy code
trackById(index: number, item: Item): number {
  return item.id; // Return unique identifier for the item
}
```

Using trackBy helps Angular track changes more efficiently and improves rendering performance.

3. Lazy Loading Modules

Lazy loading is an optimization technique that defers the loading of feature modules until they are needed. This helps reduce the initial load time of your application.

Setting Up Lazy Loading:

To implement lazy loading, define routes for lazy-loaded modules in your routing module:

```typescript
Copy code
const routes: Routes = [
  { path: 'feature', loadChildren: () =>
  import('./feature/feature.module').then(m => m.FeatureModule) },
];
```

When a user navigates to the /feature route, the FeatureModule is loaded asynchronously, improving the initial load performance of your application.

Managing Application State Efficiently

Efficient state management is crucial for maintaining high performance in Angular applications, especially as the application grows in complexity. Implementing a well-structured state management solution, such as NgRx, can help achieve this.

1. Overview of State Management with NgRx

NgRx is a state management library for Angular applications that follows the Redux pattern. It provides a robust framework for managing application state using actions, reducers, and selectors.

Key Concepts of NgRx:

- **Store**: The central repository that holds the application state. It acts as a single source of truth for the entire application.
- **Actions**: Objects that represent events in the application. Actions are dispatched to the store to indicate that something has happened.
- **Reducers**: Pure functions that specify how the application state changes in response to actions.
- **Selectors**: Functions that allow you to select specific slices of state from the store.
- **Effects**: Side effects are operations that interact with the outside world, such as making HTTP requests.

2. Setting Up NgRx

To get started with NgRx, you need to install the necessary packages and set up the store in your Angular application.

Installing NgRx Packages:

Run the following command to install NgRx:

```bash
Copy code
ng add @ngrx/store @ngrx/effects @ngrx/store-devtools
```

CHAPTER 15: BUILDING AND MAINTAINING HIGH-PERFORMANCE...

This command will install the core NgRx packages and set up the Store DevTools for debugging.

Configuring the Store:

In app.module.ts, import the necessary modules:

```typescript
Copy code
import { NgModule } from '@angular/core';
import { BrowserModule } from '@angular/platform-browser';
import { StoreModule } from '@ngrx/store';
import { EffectsModule } from '@ngrx/effects';
import { StoreDevtoolsModule } from '@ngrx/store-devtools';
import { AppComponent } from './app.component';
import { reducers } from './reducers'; // Import your reducers

@NgModule({
  declarations: [AppComponent],
  imports: [
    BrowserModule,
    StoreModule.forRoot(reducers),
    EffectsModule.forRoot([]),
    StoreDevtoolsModule.instrument({
      maxAge: 25,
      logOnly: environment.production,
    }),
  ],
  providers: [],
  bootstrap: [AppComponent],
})
export class AppModule {}
```

3. Using Selectors for Efficient State Access

Selectors allow you to retrieve specific pieces of state from the store efficiently.

Example of Creating Selectors:

Create a file named user.selectors.ts:

```typescript
Copy code
import { createFeatureSelector, createSelector } from
'@ngrx/store';
import { UserState } from './user.reducer';

export const selectUserState =
createFeatureSelector<UserState>('user');

export const selectAllUsers = createSelector(
  selectUserState,
  (state: UserState) => state.users
);

export const selectUserError = createSelector(
  selectUserState,
  (state: UserState) => state.error
);
```

Using selectors ensures that your components only subscribe to the necessary pieces of state, improving performance.

Improving Load Times

Fast load times are essential for a good user experience. Optimizing load times involves several strategies, including code splitting, preloading, and caching.

1. Code Splitting

Code splitting allows you to break your application into smaller chunks, which can be loaded on demand. Angular's lazy loading feature helps implement code splitting effectively.

Implementing Lazy Loading:

As previously mentioned, you can implement lazy loading by defining routes for lazy-loaded modules in your routing module:

CHAPTER 15: BUILDING AND MAINTAINING HIGH-PERFORMANCE...

```typescript
Copy code
const routes: Routes = [
  { path: 'feature', loadChildren: () =>
    import('./feature/feature.module').then(m => m.FeatureModule) },
];
```

When a user navigates to the /feature route, the FeatureModule is loaded asynchronously, reducing the initial load time of your application.

2. Preloading Strategies

Preloading strategies can help load lazy-loaded modules in the background after the initial load. This ensures that the user experiences minimal delay when navigating to those modules.

Example of Implementing Preloading:

You can configure preloading in your routing module:

```typescript
Copy code
import { PreloadAllModules } from '@angular/router';

const routes: Routes = [
  { path: 'feature', loadChildren: () =>
    import('./feature/feature.module').then(m => m.FeatureModule) },
];

@NgModule({
  imports: [RouterModule.forRoot(routes, { preloadingStrategy:
    PreloadAllModules })],
  exports: [RouterModule]
})
export class AppRoutingModule {}
```

By setting the preloadingStrategy to PreloadAllModules, Angular will preload all lazy-loaded modules in the background, improving perceived performance.

3. Caching Strategies

Caching can significantly improve load times and reduce server load. Implement caching for API responses and static assets.

Example of Implementing HTTP Caching:

You can implement caching for API responses using Angular's HttpClient:

```typescript
Copy code
import { Injectable } from '@angular/core';
import { HttpClient } from '@angular/common/http';
import { Observable, of } from 'rxjs';
import { tap } from 'rxjs/operators';

@Injectable({
  providedIn: 'root'
})
export class ApiService {
  private cache = new Map<string, any>();

  constructor(private http: HttpClient) {}

  getData(url: string): Observable<any> {
    if (this.cache.has(url)) {
      return of(this.cache.get(url)); // Return cached response
    } else {
      return this.http.get(url).pipe(
        tap(response => {
          this.cache.set(url, response); // Cache the response
        })
      );
    }
  }
}
```

In this example, the ApiService checks the cache before making an HTTP request. If the response is cached, it returns the cached data; otherwise, it fetches data from the API and caches the response.

Utilizing Performance Tools

Angular provides several built-in tools and features to monitor and analyze application performance. Utilizing these tools can help you identify bottlenecks and improve performance.

1. Angular DevTools

Angular DevTools is a browser extension that allows you to inspect Angular applications. It provides insights into component trees, change detection cycles, and performance profiling.

Using Angular DevTools:

1. Install the Angular DevTools extension for your browser.
2. Open your application in the browser and launch the Angular DevTools.
3. Navigate through the component tree to inspect component properties, inputs, and outputs.

2. Performance Profiling with Chrome DevTools

Chrome DevTools includes powerful performance profiling tools that allow you to analyze your application's performance in detail.

Using Chrome DevTools:

1. Open your Angular application in Chrome.
2. Press F12 to open DevTools and navigate to the "Performance" tab.
3. Click on the "Record" button and interact with your application to capture performance data.
4. Stop recording and analyze the performance metrics to identify areas for improvement.

3. Lighthouse

Lighthouse is an open-source tool for improving the quality of web pages. It provides audits for performance, accessibility, SEO, and best practices.

Running Lighthouse:

1. Open your Angular application in Chrome.
2. Press F12 to open DevTools and navigate to the "Lighthouse" tab.
3. Select the metrics you want to measure and click "Generate report."
4. Review the report to identify performance bottlenecks and areas for improvement.

Implementing Continuous Performance Monitoring

Once your application is live, continuous performance monitoring is essential for maintaining optimal performance. This involves using tools to monitor application performance, user interactions, and errors in real-time.

1. Application Performance Monitoring (APM)

APM tools allow you to monitor the performance of your application in real-time. They provide insights into application performance, including response times, transaction traces, and error rates.

Popular APM tools include:

- **New Relic**: Offers application performance monitoring, transaction tracing, and error analytics.
- **Datadog**: Provides real-time monitoring and analytics for applications and infrastructure.
- **Dynatrace**: An AI-powered APM solution that provides deep insights into application performance.

2. Error Tracking

Tracking errors in your application is crucial for maintaining performance and user experience. Implement error tracking tools to capture and analyze errors in real-time.

Popular error tracking tools include:

- **Sentry**: Monitors and reports errors in real-time, providing insights into the stack trace and context.
- **Rollbar**: Offers error monitoring and alerting, allowing you to identify

and fix issues quickly.

- **LogRocket**: Captures user sessions and logs errors, providing insights into user interactions leading to issues.

Conclusion

In this chapter, we covered essential strategies for building and maintaining high-performance Angular applications. We explored techniques for optimizing rendering performance, managing application state, improving load times, and utilizing caching. Additionally, we discussed the importance of continuous performance monitoring and implementing security best practices.

By applying these strategies, you can create Angular applications that are not only fast and responsive but also secure and reliable. This knowledge positions you as a proficient Angular developer, capable of tackling complex projects and delivering high-quality applications that meet user expectations.

Conclusion

As we reach the end of this comprehensive exploration of Angular development, it's important to reflect on the journey we've undertaken. This book has provided a detailed roadmap for mastering Angular 16 and ASP.NET Core 7.0 development, from the foundational concepts to advanced techniques. The knowledge gained here empowers developers to build robust, scalable, and high-performance applications while adhering to best practices for security and maintainability.

1. Recap of Key Concepts

Throughout this book, we have covered a wide range of topics, each designed to equip you with the necessary skills and understanding to navigate the complex landscape of modern web development. Here are some of the key concepts we explored:

Understanding Angular and ASP.NET Core

- **Framework Foundations**: We started by establishing a solid understanding of Angular as a powerful front-end framework and ASP.NET Core as a versatile back-end technology. Their synergy allows developers to create full-stack applications with efficiency and scalability.
- **Component-Based Architecture**: Angular's component-based architecture promotes reusability, encapsulation, and separation of concerns, enabling developers to manage complex UIs effectively.

CONCLUSION

Development Environment Setup

- **Setting Up the Environment**: We discussed the prerequisites for Angular and ASP.NET Core development, including installing necessary tools like Visual Studio, Node.js, and Angular CLI, and configuring the development environment for optimal productivity.

Building Web APIs and Angular Applications

- **Creating RESTful APIs**: You learned how to design and implement RESTful APIs using ASP.NET Core, enabling seamless communication between the front end and back end.
- **Building Angular Applications**: We walked through the process of creating Angular applications, including setting up components, services, and routing, as well as leveraging Angular features such as directives and dependency injection.

State Management and Performance Optimization

- **Managing State with NgRx**: We explored NgRx as a robust state management solution for Angular applications, emphasizing the importance of a centralized store for maintaining application state efficiently.
- **Optimizing Performance**: Techniques for optimizing rendering performance, reducing load times, and implementing caching strategies were discussed in detail, helping you ensure a responsive user experience.

Security Best Practices

- **Securing Angular Applications**: The importance of implementing robust security measures to protect applications from vulnerabilities was emphasized. We covered authentication, authorization, and strategies for mitigating common attacks like XSS and CSRF.

Continuous Improvement and Monitoring

- **Implementing Continuous Monitoring**: We highlighted the significance of performance monitoring and error tracking tools that allow you to maintain high-performance standards and quickly address issues as they arise.

2. The Importance of Continued Learning

Web development is a dynamic field that evolves rapidly. New technologies, frameworks, and best practices emerge frequently. To remain competitive and effective as a developer, it's essential to commit to lifelong learning. Here are some strategies to keep your skills sharp:

- **Stay Updated**: Follow the official Angular blog, subscribe to newsletters, and join relevant communities to keep abreast of the latest updates and features in Angular and ASP.NET Core.
- **Engage with the Community**: Participate in forums, attend meetups, and contribute to open-source projects. Engaging with the developer community can provide valuable insights and networking opportunities.
- **Practice and Experiment**: Continuously build projects that challenge your skills. Experiment with new features, libraries, and tools to gain hands-on experience and deepen your understanding.
- **Explore Related Technologies**: Expand your knowledge beyond Angular and ASP.NET Core. Familiarize yourself with complementary technologies such as TypeScript, GraphQL, and Progressive Web Apps (PWAs).

3. Embracing Best Practices

Throughout this book, we emphasized the importance of adhering to best practices in development. Implementing best practices not only enhances the quality and maintainability of your code but also fosters collaboration among team members and improves the overall development process.

- **Code Quality**: Write clean, maintainable code by following established coding standards and conventions. Utilize tools like linters and formatters to enforce consistency.
- **Testing**: Implement comprehensive testing strategies, including unit tests, integration tests, and end-to-end tests. A robust testing suite ensures that your applications behave as expected and minimizes the risk of regressions.
- **Documentation**: Maintain clear and concise documentation for your code, APIs, and application architecture. Good documentation is invaluable for onboarding new team members and facilitating collaboration.

4. Looking Ahead: The Future of Angular Development

As Angular continues to evolve, it's essential to stay informed about upcoming features and enhancements. Here are some trends and developments to watch for in the Angular ecosystem:

- **Improved Performance**: Future versions of Angular are likely to introduce optimizations and enhancements aimed at improving performance, reducing bundle sizes, and enhancing developer productivity.
- **Enhanced Tooling**: The Angular CLI and related tools will continue to evolve, offering new features and improvements to streamline the development process.
- **Integration with Emerging Technologies**: Angular's compatibility with technologies such as serverless architectures, microservices, and GraphQL will likely become more pronounced, allowing developers to create modern applications that leverage these advancements.
- **Community-Driven Development**: The Angular community plays a significant role in shaping the framework's future. Engage with community discussions and contribute to the evolution of Angular through feedback and participation.

5. Final Thoughts

Building applications using Angular and ASP.NET Core is an exciting and rewarding journey. With the knowledge and skills you have gained from this book, you are well-equipped to tackle real-world projects and create applications that are not only functional but also performant and secure.

Remember that the key to success in software development lies in adaptability, continuous learning, and a commitment to excellence. Embrace challenges as opportunities for growth, and never hesitate to seek help and collaboration from the vibrant developer community.

As you move forward in your Angular development journey, I encourage you to apply the principles and practices outlined in this book. By doing so, you will not only enhance your skills but also contribute positively to the ever-evolving world of web development.

6. Appendix: Resources for Further Learning

To support your continued learning and development in Angular and ASP.NET Core, here are some valuable resources:

Books

- **"Angular Up & Running" by Shyam Seshadri**: A practical guide to building robust Angular applications.
- **"Pro ASP.NET Core 6" by Adam Freeman**: A comprehensive resource for building applications using ASP.NET Core.
- **"Learning Angular" by Brad Dayley, Brendan Dayley, and Caleb Dayley**: An accessible introduction to Angular development.

Online Courses

- **Angular - The Complete Guide (2023 Edition)** on Udemy: A comprehensive course covering all aspects of Angular development.
- **ASP.NET Core Fundamentals** on Pluralsight: A foundational course for

ASP.NET Core development.

Community and Forums

- **Stack Overflow**: A popular platform for asking questions and sharing knowledge with the developer community.
- **Angular Forum**: A dedicated forum for Angular developers to discuss topics and share insights.
- **Reddit - r/Angular**: A community of Angular developers sharing news, tips, and resources.

www.ingramcontent.com/pod-product-compliance
Lightning Source LLC
Chambersburg PA
CBHW071020240526
45469CB00006BD/2005